TWELVE MONTHS OF SUNDAYS

Reflections on Bible Readings, Year B

TWELVE MONTHS OF SUNDAYS

Reflections on Bible Readings, Year B

N. T. WRIGHT

SPCK

Published in Great Britain in 2002 by
Society for Promoting Christian Knowledge
Holy Trinity Church
Marylebone Road
London NW1 4DU

British Library Cataloguing-in-Publication Data
A catalogue record for this book
is available from the British Library

ISBN 0-281-05289-1

Typeset by Wilmaset Ltd, Birkenhead, Wirral
Printed in Great Britain by
The Cromwell Press, Trowbridge, Wiltshire

TWELVE MONTHS OF SUNDAYS

N. T. Wright is Canon Theologian of Westminster Abbey, and holds the degree of Doctor of Divinity from Oxford University and an honorary DD from Aberdeen University. He taught New Testament Studies in Cambridge, Montreal and Oxford, and worked as a college chaplain, before becoming Dean of Lichfield in 1994 and moving to Westminster in 2000. He has written over thirty books about the origins of Christianity and its contemporary relevance. Dr Wright broadcasts regularly on radio and television. He is married with four young adult children.

Contents

— ≈ —

Preface

—— ∼ ——

This is the third and last collection of my reflections on the weekly biblical readings in the official lectionary now used in the Church of England. Almost all the pieces appeared originally in the *Church Times*, and I am grateful for the encouragement of many readers to give them this secondary lease of life.

The present volume covers Year B of the three-year cycle, which will come into use in Advent 2002 and every third year thereafter. The readings are set out in *The Christian Year* (Church House Publishing, 1997). I have added extra pieces so that all the 'Propers' are covered, however early or late Easter may be. I have not, though, attempted to cover any of the saints' days or other festivals that may from time to time fall on, or be transferred to, a Sunday. I have used the 'continuous' set of readings for the Sundays in Ordinary Time after Trinity, as opposed to the 'related' ones.

I assume that the reader will have a Bible to hand, or preferably more than one, since comparing translations is often a good way to generate fresh reflection. These pieces, after all, are designed as matches to light one's own candle with, not candles in their own right; they are to stimulate, not to stifle, one's own grappling with the text. As I review these comments two years after they were originally written, I am struck both by the inexhaustible range and richness of the Bible and by the depressing sense that the Church, though sitting on such a goldmine, appears to get little joy or energy from it. Albert Schweitzer spoke in another context of someone who insisted on bringing water for his garden from a long distance in a leaky bucket, despite the fact that there was a running stream close at hand. The Church is often tempted to go to all sorts of faraway places for advice, energy, hope and even faith; but the sparkling stream of scripture, even the small amount piped in through the lectionary week by week, is well able not only to refresh us but also to water the gardens we haven't yet thought of planting.

Once again I express thanks to Paul Handley, Editor of the *Church Times*, and to the editorial staff at SPCK. This time, though, it is a delight to thank Yolande Clarke for double duty: having overseen the original pieces for the *Church Times*, she has now processed them again for SPCK. Her keen editorial eye has been a great help; her cheerful patience, even when I overstepped deadlines for the hundredth time, deserves a medal.

N. T. Wright
Candlemas 2002

Advent

The First Sunday of Advent

— ∾ —

Isaiah 64.1–9
1 Corinthians 1.3–9
Mark 13.24–37

Advent has stolen the old Christmas mystique. The symbolism of darkness awaiting dawn makes sense in a post-modern world where Christmas razzmatazz has been debunked, demythologized and deconstructed. Hope in the night, not glitzy commercialism, is what we want and need.

This is a deeply biblical move. Cut Christmas out of the Bible, and you lose three chapters (the doctrine of the incarnation hardly hinges on it, as the evidence of Paul makes clear). Try cutting Advent, and you lose half the Old Testament and most of the New. Jews and Christians have always, though in a wide variety of ways, lived within and by the story of God's order appearing within the world's confusion, God's fiery light burning away the shadows. The New Testament re-uses the Old Testament language and imagery of God's breaking into world history, not least 'the day of the Lord', to speak of what will happen on 'the day of our Lord Jesus Christ'. Get Advent right, and you will find Christology comes along with it.

But why? And what are we to hope *for*? Advent has its equivalents of shepherds and wise men, and perhaps also of Father Christmas – the walk-on parts that can all too easily get in the way of deeper understanding. Clouds, trumpets, angels, cosmic catastrophe – a Christian version of *Star Wars* and *Apocalypse Now*, easily beguiling us into thinking that it's all make-believe.

It isn't. It speaks of the time when the thin but opaque curtain that hangs in the midst of reality, the bright veil between heaven and earth, will be ripped aside. Our present reality, existing – did we but know it – a hair's breadth away from the terror and splendour of God, would be confronted with that other Reality, setting the cosmos burning and bubbling, calling forth the deepest shame ('we are all unclean') and the most intimate hope ('yet, Lord, you are our Father'). Afraid of shame, we are often ready to trade in hope if only we can be left without such an Advent.

We can't. It's already happened. What we ought to celebrate at Christmas, instead of wrapping it tightly in trivia to prevent the glory bursting out, is the story of heaven opened, glory unveiled, God's shame and intimacy meeting ours. Advent, rather than the recently introduced pre-Advent 'Kingdom season', is the end of the church year, as well as the beginning. Those who await the final unveiling of God's majesty and love are to be sustained by meditating on its first mysterious appearing.

Yes, and by waiting in readiness. Jesus' warnings about the imminent fall of Jerusalem resonate into subsequent history. The shame which befell the unbelieving city points ahead to a yet greater shame. The watchful hope of Jesus' loyal followers calls us to further vigilance. To believe in God's future is to see why it is vital to stay alert and take action in the present. Christmas has become cosy. Advent calls us to stay awake.

The Second Sunday of Advent

—— ~ ——

Isaiah 40.1–11
2 Peter 3.8–15a
Mark 1.1–8

If John the Baptist was going to raise up the valleys and flatten out the mountains, he started in the right place. Jericho lies a long way below the road-sign that says 'sea level'; Jerusalem, a long way above. Topography won't matter when YHWH returns.

Nor will the transience of the rest of the natural order, including not only grass but human beings. What matters is God's Word. The later Christian inclination to take all references to God's Word to refer to the Bible itself is understandable but limiting. God's self-disclosing, self-expressing being goes forth powerfully, emerging in prophetic oracles old and new, creating new worlds and new people to match and inhabit the new day that God's return to Zion will bring about.

All this can of course be said of scripture, when rightly handled. It remains living and active. But the image here is not of a book, safe and domesticated (as we so easily suppose) on a shelf, but of the authoritative word which called into being the first creation and now brings forth the new one, the 'new heavens and new earth' that still form the stuff of Christian hope. This is why Isaiah's herald has something to shout about.

Isaiah combines what we find it so hard to: majesty and

4

comfort. The more authoritative our God-picture, the more we find it difficult to speak at the same time of tender comfort for the long-term prisoner (v. 2) or of gentle leading of lambs and mother sheep (v. 11). The message of the Baptist, too, seems more at home with the other pole of Isaianic language, the imperious command to clear a path for the Mighty One, whose arm rules for him, who brings rewards and recompense. Yet part of the point of Mark's picture of John, and part of the paradox of John's whole career, is precisely that when he spoke of the Mightier One (perhaps evoking Isaiah 40.10) we look around and see Jesus. It is like that moment in Revelation 5 when, looking for a lion, we discover a lamb.

And in that Lamb God's glory has been revealed, for all flesh to see together. We easily think of 'glory' as meaning 'luminosity', but this, though often implied as well, is not its primary denotation. 'Glory' is what you see when the inner truth of God is revealed, when God's own very self is known, not misunderstood or distorted but recognized as what it is, and so loved and adored.

Mark is telling us, by the very framing of his story (even if, as some suppose, his own opening has been lost, leaving us with a rather abrupt editorial introduction), that this is what we will see in Jesus of Nazareth. 2 Peter reminds us that, within the tumultuous and world-shaking events of which prophecy and Gospel speak, we are to remember the loving patience of the Lord, and to see in that our salvation.

The Third Sunday of Advent

———— ∾ ————

Isaiah 61.1–4, 8–11
1 Thessalonians 5.16–24
John 1.6–8, 19–28

Restrain the impulse towards Isaiah's rolling cadences and
John's pregnant simplicity, and ponder what Paul has packed
into such a small space. Apart from verse 23 (a benediction
for those awaiting the Lord's presence), the rest of this nine-
verse passage is very clipped. No argument; no discourse;
only one explanatory phrase; eight commands; a concluding
promise. Forty-one words in the Greek, just over five per
verse. Blessed is the one who ponders each, and the way in
which they bring the Advent hope into present reality.

First, celebration. 'Rejoice always'; easy to caricature, but
easy too to miss the point. Present celebration is rooted in
what has already been achieved in Christ, and what is
thereby guaranteed.

Second, ceaseless prayer. Easier said than done, we think,
and settle for less than one hour in 24; yet Paul was busy too,
had much to be anxious about, and could still speak of
anticipating here and now the life of heaven.

Gratitude in all circumstances: Paul's were more trying
than most, yet one hint of trouble and we back off, despite
his interesting explanation. Gratitude, it seems, is at the heart
of the genuine humanness not only modelled but given to us
in Christ; it is, again, a key sign of living in the present in the
light of the promised future. These first three commands, like

the opening clauses in the Lord's Prayer, are all about looking to God and God's future.

We then have two commands to be open to fresh winds of the Spirit: don't quench the Spirit, don't despise prophesying. New wine is inconvenient in church, embarrassing even; but unless God is doing new things how can we be living as future-oriented people?

Finally, three commands to serious moral decisions. Test everything; cling tight to what is good (if you don't, it'll slip out of your fingers); back off from everything that even looks evil. God's future judgement is to work forwards into appropriate moral seriousness. Again, there are echoes of the Lord's Prayer. Was this, perhaps, the kind of quick teaching Paul would give his converts at a very basic stage? Have we improved on it?

Finally, the promise: he who calls you is faithful, and will accomplish it. A beloved aunt wrote the first three Greek words, *pistos ho kalon*, on a card for my confirmation, and I have it still, all these years later. The future assured action of the Lord undergirds the future-oriented behaviour of the disciple. Like John the Baptist, so preoccupied with what (and who) was coming that all he could do was to point away from himself and towards God's future, we are to pray, dance, and be holy, for tomorrow we live.

Now place this brief picture of Christian behaviour within the majestic promises and flights of imagery of Isaiah 61. Sit back and enjoy the ride. But remember: in an aeroplane, the nuts and bolts are just as important as the wings.

The Fourth Sunday of Advent

——— ⁓ ———

2 Samuel 7.1–11, 16
Romans 16.25–7
Luke 1.26–38

It always was a mystery. Not just a puzzle – there are enough of those as well, God knows – but a genuine mystery, a truth whose parallel lines disappear behind God's dark curtain, to meet in that infinity of truth where all is literal and all is metaphorical. Did God intend Israel to have a king? Read 1 Samuel 8 and ponder. Did God intend Israel to have a temple? Read 2 Samuel 7 again and ponder.

At one level they seem simply concessions to Israel's desire to be like everyone else. A king, like all the nations; a temple, like the ones up the road. There's the problem: borrowing light from the world, instead of being the light *of* the world. Kings become corrupt, and are exiled (beginning with David himself, whose immorality, copied among his children, leads to Absalom's rebellion). Temples become first idols, then ruins.

And yet. God desires justice and mercy for his people, not unredeemed anarchy. God desires to dwell among his people, not to remain distant. A king after God's own heart? A temple that is simultaneously movable and appropriate to God's majesty?

The ambiguities of this double dream converge on the apparently jokey pun in 2 Samuel 7.11 (do read verses 12–15 as well; I know the lectionary is trying to stimulate us to fresh

8

thought, but we have enough puzzles without home-made ones). David wants to build God a house; God promises that he will build David a 'house' – a son who will be God's own son, whose Davidic throne will be established for ever.

Why did God change the subject? Had he forgotten David's suggestion about a temple? No. There was an appropriate way for the living, loving God to dwell in the midst of his people: the stone temple would point the way towards it, but would remain an ambiguous signpost. The reality would be a human being, reflecting God's image; a king, embodying God's wise ordering of the people; a man after God's own heart, whose heart would be broken by the pain of the world but who would in that moment render all man-made temples redundant.

No wonder, as Paul says, that this is a mystery hidden long ago and only disclosed in Jesus. (Paul's language tumbles over itself in getting to the end of his great letter, but the confusion – is the glory going to God, or to Jesus, or both? – is thoroughly appropriate.) Mary becomes the temporary dwelling-place of the living God: the presence of the Holy Spirit, and the 'overshadowing' of the Most High, both evoke the temple-idea. This passage struggles to say something for which words hardly exist: that in Mary's womb temple and king came together once and for all, that the scriptures came true in ways never imagined, and that God found at last the house, neither tent nor temple but flesh and blood, that would most truly and fully express his royal, self-giving love.

Christmas

The First Sunday of Christmas

—— ∾ ——

Isaiah 61.10—62.3
Galatians 4.4–7
Luke 2.15–21

God sent the Son ... and God sent the Spirit of the Son. St Paul brings together Christmas and Pentecost – as unlikely a pair, to our culture-conditioned minds, as plum pudding and a May Bank Holiday. Son and Spirit remain inseparable. Ask Mary.

Paul is describing how slaves become God's adopted children and heirs. Telling, as so often, a fresh variation on the story of the Exodus, he sees the law itself as the instrument of slavery. It locked up the Jews in condemnation; it locked out the Gentiles from membership. Is God then powerless to keep his promise to Abraham, the promise of a worldwide family?

No. The birth of the child, as with Abraham himself, signals God's faithfulness, God's grace breaking through human impossibility. Born of a woman, born under the law, the Messiah has come to the slave-market, and has purchased his people's freedom. Christmas people are to think of themselves as Passover people, and then also as Pentecost people: what God did in the birth of the one child, God now does in the birth of dozens, thousands, tens of millions in whose hearts the Spirit is poured out, and on whose lips is the newborn cry, 'Abba, Father'. ('Abba' isn't just a child's word, but here it is treated as the sure sign of new life.) Father, Son and Spirit: God's inner life, shared with us all.

Come back to Bethlehem, therefore, and see what has come to pass. Only come now, with the angels singing, and see not one babe in the manger, but more than anyone could count: children and heirs of the free love of God, Passover people, Pentecost people. Christmas is the time of celebration because this new birth heralds all new birth. In this young son all God's Exodus people are called to be sons and daughters, free heirs of God's lavish grace, clothed (as Isaiah says) with the garments of salvation. If we are in danger of becoming blasé about Christmas, we may run the risk of becoming complacent also about the miracle of the Spirit's work, perhaps for similar reasons. We know the story too well, and have stopped pondering it in our hearts.

'Pondering' is a powerful word in the original. It isn't just puzzled musing or focused daydreaming. It speaks of bringing together, or even throwing together, a collection of people, ideas or objects, and seeing what happens. Like the sages and visionaries of old, Mary guarded great and terrible secrets in her heart, turning them this way and that, letting them knock sparks off each other. God and the farm-hands. Angels and straw. Grace and blood. Journeys and lodgings and babies and prayers. In and through them all, for her and for us, there weaves the story of God's unexpected love and power, setting the whole to a music at once strange, wild and redemptive, a Magnificat that now heralds each new birth, each Spirit-led baby-cry, each new personal Christmas.

The Second Sunday of Christmas

—— ~ ——

Jeremiah 31.7–14
Ephesians 1.3–14
John 1.[1–9] 10–18

'He gave them the right to become children of God,' says John. 'I have become a father to Israel,' says God to Jeremiah, 'and Ephraim is my firstborn.' 'He destined us for adoption as his children,' says Paul. Exodus-imagery, of course: Israel's status as God's firstborn, announced to Pharaoh as the reason for freeing Israel from slavery, will be reaffirmed through covenant renewal (Jeremiah), and has been so reaffirmed in Jesus (John and Paul).

These writers are not primarily concerned about status. They are celebrating actual knowledge of God: first-hand, intimate, astonishing knowledge that swept them off their feet and left them unable to keep silent. Jeremiah had witnessed the depth of self-caused suffering of those who turned from the living God to idols; now, in a sustained two-chapter poem, he invites us to gaze at fresh-minted promises springing from sheer grace. Israel has no merit or innate worth to cause the covenant God to replace the judgement of exile with the assurance of new delight. These lavish promises, worth pondering every new day, let alone every new year, let alone every new century, spring from love, and love alone: not from the will of the flesh, nor from the will of man, but from God.

Jeremiah's words are flesh-words: words of singing, of

14

exiles returning home, of shepherds with flocks, of grain and wine and oil. Eden will come again; young and old will celebrate together. Nor should we write the flesh-dimension out of the celebration when we turn to Ephesians. The 'inheritance' has been transformed from a single country to the whole world (compare Romans 8). But the entire paean of praise (verses 3–14 are a single sentence in the Greek) remains earthed – the metaphor is appropriate – in the Jewish tradition, with its unreserved celebration of God's goodness in creation.

The blessings are called 'spiritual', and we already have them 'in the heavenly places', but that is simply their present mode and location. Everything in heaven and earth is being summed up in the Messiah (v. 10), himself the truly human one, to whom, as in creation's original intention, all is now subject (vv. 20–23). God's eventual design is for a single heaven/earth reality; Jeremiah will recognize in it the things he was talking about. And in Christ, once more, all is given as a gift of grace, not accomplished by the will of the flesh, nor by the will of man, but by God.

The kaleidoscope of grace thus reveals ever-new glimpses of a glory in which the delights of creation are caught up within the larger purposes of God. This God, known and experienced now as the Father-God, the Exodus-God, is discovered – and if we aren't regularly surprised by this something has gone wrong – in his perfect image, the flesh-word, God the Only Son. Grace upon grace. Re-set the calendar by that basic principle, and who knows what might follow?

Epiphany

The First Sunday of Epiphany

—— ～ ——

Genesis 1.1–5
Acts 19.1–7
Mark 1.4–11

Wind and water. Light and dark. Heaven and earth. The beginning.

There is a quiet joy about the opening of Genesis. Quiet, not because it's only slightly exciting, but because we know at once that these are the soft opening notes of a theme that will grow and swell, rise and develop, until the whole orchestra has joined in with wild, exuberant harmony and counterpoint. Even that will only be the completion of the beginning. God saw that it was good. But there is more.

The wind of God sweeps over the waters. Difficult to know how much to hear in that phrase. 'Wind' is the same Hebrew word as 'spirit', or even 'Spirit'; there is a good deal to be said for thinking that the writer, editor(s) and transmitters of Genesis 1 would not have made the finicky post-Enlightenment distinctions that we do. A full range of meaning is available, from 'a mighty wind' through to 'God's Spirit'. The wind blows where it wills, and we don't know its origin or destination; so it often is with meaning. Best to spread sail and be carried along.

Not for nothing do we find John the Baptist in the Johannine prologue, up there along with light and life, part of the new Genesis. As Mark makes clear, John's baptism is a signal of new creation: he appears as a prophet, a sign of

18

renewal and restoration, both in his garb, his diet, his location, his message and his very person. Forgiveness of sins was not just what everyone knew they needed person-ally; it was what Israel needed, because unforgiven sin was directly correlated in the corporate consciousness with the present parlous state of Israel's national fortunes. The meaning of a royal pardon is not simply that the prisoner enjoys a good feeling of innocence restored, but that he gets out of jail.

Scarcely surprising that we find disciples of John in Turkey 25 years later. His message had spread far and wide. But you can't stop with John. Just as Genesis moves forward, so does the story of which John knows himself to be a part. He prepares the water and invokes the Spirit, through which will come the judgement which is also mercy, the new Day which will show up the Night as 'darkness'. (Notice how God saw that the light was good, and separated it from the darkness; think what that might have meant to a first-century Jew.) Then it happens. A figure emerges from the water. Heaven and earth are suddenly present to each other. Wind becomes Spirit, Spirit becomes dove; every section of the orchestra takes up the theme, and over it all is heard a solo voice. My son. My beloved. My delight.

God saw that it was good. What does he see now, at the start of a new year? Where are the signs of new creation? Where are the dark, formless voids that still await the rushing mighty wind?

The Second Sunday of Epiphany

—— ❧ ——

1 Samuel 3.1–10 [11–20]
Revelation 5.1–10
John 1.43–51

The word of the Lord was rare in Eli's day. The scroll remained sealed until the Lamb appeared. Nathanael sat under his fig tree, unknown, undisturbed. Not because God couldn't speak or didn't care, but because his foolishness is wiser, as always, than human wisdom. A voice in the night at Shiloh. A man from Nazareth, the town from which no good comes. A Lamb that had been slain. The strange stamp of authenticity.

Eli, old, blind and no longer in control, still recognizes the source and the method, even though the new word brings judgement on his family. 'It is YHWH; let him do what seems good to him.' The previous chapter chronicles the disobedience of his sons, the growth of Samuel, and the earlier warnings. Now the scene is set for the new thing Israel's God will do, and it will begin with the word, initially misunderstood but finally unmistakable: a gentle repeated call, demanding that Samuel first listen and then speak. That rhythm of costly obedience, learnt in a night and sustained through a lifetime, sets a pattern for prophetic ministry then and now. Where are today's Samuels? Have they the courage to tell Eli what they have heard?

From the shrine at Shiloh to the heavenly court. John the Seer, like a Hebrew prophet of old, stands as an onlooker in the divine council. He is called to report back to his fellow-mortals what he has seen. Within that, he is called to long for God's purposes to come to pass and to grieve if they appear thwarted. But then the Lamb is given the right, because of his redeeming death, to open the seven-sealed scroll. He has created a new people, destined to be priest-kings in God's coming kingdom. God's will shall be done, on earth as in heaven.

This vision of 'heaven' is not a forward glance to a final non-earthly destiny. It is a glimpse of the *present* time in God's dimension of reality; and in that present time God's plans for the future are stored up, waiting to be unrolled. God's kingdom will come, through the victory of the Lamb, 'on earth' (v. 10), not just in heaven. The rest of the book, not least its climax in chapters 21—2, will confirm this.

Fresh revelation, for which the Church should pray and wait and pore over scripture, is a matter of a window opening, a bridge being created, between the heavenly and earthly dimensions. Jesus' banter with Nathanael, each seeming to test the other out but with Jesus retaining the initiative, suddenly gives way to a promise of just such prophetic vision. Jacob's ladder, joining heaven and earth, is replaced by the Son of Man himself, not only a Messianic figure (v. 51 confirming vv. 45 and 49) but the one through whom the heavenly throne-room is glimpsed, the divine purpose is accomplished. The Word of God comes again, calling the world to fresh allegiance.

The Third Sunday of Epiphany

———— ∿ ————

Genesis 14.17–20
Revelation 19.6–10
John 2.1–11

Considering how many symbolic themes John has woven together here, it is remarkable that the story remains clear and powerful. Like a great Shakespearean speech, it simultaneously drives us forward and urges us to pause and ponder.

Strike each of these bells, and see what echoes are set off. The third day. A wedding. More wine needed. Purification-pots. Glory revealed.

Weddings spoke of God's coming kingdom, as they still do in Jesus' parables and in the closing chapters of Revelation. Wine recalls the salvation-feast in Isaiah 25, as well as the strange refreshment Melchizedek offered Abram. Jesus' 'hour' has not yet come, but with this action the clock moves forward another minute. Water tells of life, the Spirit, new birth. Within the Jewish purification-rites, and without Messianic intervention, water is available but not lifegiving; salvation is of the Jews, but for the world. The last-minute new wine speaks of new creation, coming at last through the Word made flesh. And so on. In this story at least, when the reader discovers allegorical significance the chances are the author intended it.

John's summary points on to the final disclosure of glory. This is the first sign; more will follow, in a sequential crescendo. As a good writer, John reminds us of this only once (4.54). When we reach 12.37 we realize we should have been counting; with 13.1 the hour has struck; and by 20.30 we understand that the last signs, the final unveiling of glory, have occurred in Calvary and Easter. Only then do we fully grasp what was going on at Cana in Galilee.

Only then, for instance, do we see the full picture of Jesus and his mother. She longs for him to be the Messiah she had imagined; as here, he both is and isn't. He fulfils Israel's hopes, but in a new way. Think of her in this story (as the beloved disciple must have thought of her) as the woman who will stand, still uncomprehending, at the foot of the cross: Lady, what have you to do with me? Why put me on the spot? What did you expect? She has both understood and misunderstood. She must travel the long road, and wait in darkness for the hour to strike.

Like the wedding itself, she becomes a symbol, rushing to Jesus wanting instant solutions. The answer may be given, and will point on to more yet to come; but Jesus is not there at our beck and call to smooth over social embarrassments, to make water into wine as required, or to square inconvenient circles. He is there to reveal God's glory. Like Mary, we must learn where, and how, that will take place.

And, like the servants, we must obey even when the order seems bizarre or even plain daft. Fancy risking your job, and the steward's anger, by serving purification-water on the say-so of a stranger. Fancy disobeying and missing the glory.

The Fourth Sunday of Epiphany

——— ～ ———

Deuteronomy 18.15–20
Revelation 12.1–5a
Mark 1.21–28

Authority, so problematic for us, is central to the biblical message. The Kingdom of God is not a democracy, as a character in *Chariots of Fire* pointed out. When the Israelites banded together to decide things their own way, they voted either to go back to Egypt or to make a golden calf. Almost the only time the apostles acted unanimously was when 'they all forsook him and fled'. God's redemptive word of authority, calling us to order, breaks through the noise of humans stampeding in the wrong direction. Admitting this means swallowing pride. Refusing to recognize it means conniving at self-destruction. Lemmings all go together when they go.

And yet. We learnt long ago that power corrupts; we learnt more recently that all authority is to be distrusted. Humanly speaking these are important lessons. Yet one can no more live on suspicion than one can eat a Marxist tract. Without trust breaking through afresh we condemn ourselves to bleak, cynical lives. Trustworthy authority appears, as a strange gift from God, so that we may find the way forward out of our self-imposed prison.

Of course, the costs of freedom sometimes make us shrink back. Notice how the destructive, dehumanizing 'unclean spirit' shrieks out its accusation that it is the one being destroyed. Truth is an early victim in spiritual warfare, as in other kinds. The new teaching, 'with authority' (as Jesus' onlookers remark with surprise), comes to cut through the shroud of lies, to announce the presence of the living, life-giving God, the only one in whose name a true prophet will speak, and to declare the victory of this God over the ancient dragon.

Turn this scenario into lurid apocalyptic dream-language, and you have Revelation 12 in a nutshell (though why one should break the paragraph before verse 6 is a mystery). Many cultures told tales of a young prince, born to destroy the old tyrant, spirited away until the final battle lest the tyrant strike first. First-century Rome told a story (not least through images on coins, the main mass medium of that society) of the resplendent goddess Roma giving birth to the young emperor who would rule the whole world, defeating all rivals. The early Christians adapted the first of these, and showed up the second as a ghastly parody of the truth.

In the Christian story, replete with biblical echoes (e.g. of Psalm 2.9), the old tyrant is the satan, the accuser. Rome becomes the agent of evil, not the redeemer. And Jesus, born from within the messianic community, is destined to over-throw not only all arrogant human authority but all destruc-tive spiritual forces as well.

True authority is thus the liberating rule of the woman's child. The idea that all authority is suspect turns out to be the last great lie of the jailer. But if valid authority is revealed in Jesus, its shape and goal are very different from what we have come to expect.

Ordinary Time

Proper 1

—— ⁓ ——

Isaiah 40.21–31
1 Corinthians 9.16–23
Mark 1.29–39

Nobody in Corinth had seen it before. Nobody had *thought* of it. It wasn't on their mental map, any more than it is in our world. So when Paul wanted to tell them that as Christians, working out how to live in a pagan environment, they might face times when they should voluntarily forgo something to which they had a complete right – an intricate but vital principle – the only example he could give of what this might look like was his own.

Hence this bit of autobiography, providing a fascinating glimpse of both Paul's practice and his theory. The under-lying point (chapters 8, 10) concerns food offered to idols. Christians, believing in the creator God, are free to eat whatever is sold in the market. But because they believe in this God through the crucified Jesus, their freedom is further defined by the gospel's confrontation with evil, and by the conscience of fellow-believers. They must not give offence.

The equivalent point in Paul's regular practice is poignant in context: he has refrained from charging the Corinthians financially for his services as an apostle. He claims the right to such support, but voluntarily does without it, in order to spread the gospel as widely as possible. The same rule has governed his behaviour when faced with different groups in society: he will voluntarily submit to their social customs

while among them, not because his own salvation depends
upon it but because theirs may. Those who today take the
gospel into fresh territory, geographical or social, will need
to work out the equivalent in each case.

They may also need to think out answers to the inevitable
charge of inconsistency. Being loyal to the gospel seems to
mean being prepared to appear disloyal from time to time to
what seem to others like principles. Distinguishing this
position in turn from currently fashionable relativism may
be one of the great moral challenges of our time.

The flurry of activity on a single busy Sabbath in Capernaum no doubt raised similar questions both for the towns-
people and for Jesus' initial disciples. What was going on?
Where would it lead? Was Capernaum now to be the centre
of a new movement of healing and teaching? Everybody was
looking for Jesus; a few more days, and the whole town
would have been on his side. But he had to move on. Other
places needed to hear. The gospel took precedence over
human success and even human stability. Another hard
lesson, now as then.

Underneath the hard lessons we find the unshakeable trust
of both Jesus and Paul in the purposes of the one true God.
Human traditions and structures were as nothing compared
to the sovereignty and supremacy of this God. Isaiah's
majestic vision of God, dwarfing both the stars of the
heavens and the princes of the earth, remains an excellent
starting-point for living in God's presence, and for pondering
what the gospel demands of, and assures to, those who
announce it.

Proper 2

—— ≈ ——

2 Kings 5.1–14
1 Corinthians 9.24–27
Mark 1.40–45

Naaman's wife's maid knew more about Elisha's healing powers than the king of Israel. All the king could do was tear his clothes and rage against his Syrian counterpart, suspecting that a request for healing was a disguised excuse for renewed hostility in their already long-running, and still continuing, border disputes. In such a setting, a concession or a friendly request or gesture is instantly regarded with suspicion. As we know, three thousand years of tussling over territory is not easily forgotten.

Could Naaman's own story – including the verses after our passage ends – indicate ways forward? He, too, one of the great ones in that little world, has to learn from his servants what he could not see for himself: that the humiliation which leads to health is better than the pride which leaves you a leper. The rivers of Damascus were indeed greater than the muddy stream of Jordan, but they had never parted to let God's people through to the promised land. They could not serve as symbols of new life.

Naaman's conclusion is striking, now as then: there is no God in all the earth except in Israel (v. 15). No other god does this sort of thing. But if the outsider Naaman can be welcomed and healed, the insider Gehazi, who behaves like a shameless pagan, is thrust out. Humiliation and pride know no boundaries; judgement, like mercy, is applied even-handedly by the one true God. Those who grasp all they can will find that it chokes them. Those who humble themselves will find healing. The self-control of which Paul speaks is required in full measure at this point, both in personal and communal life.

Mark's description of Jesus' confrontation with a leper is puzzling, particularly v. 43. Some translations soften it, but it looks as though Jesus is overcome with fierce emotion. Has the leper taunted him, challenging him with a harder act of healing than his previous ones (perhaps ruled out by v. 41)? Is it that Jesus suspects the leper is deliberately approaching him as if he were a king (he kneels to him, v. 40)? Is it because such a healing will now let the cat out of the bag, inviting attention on a scale Jesus had not wanted, or not this soon? Or is Jesus, perhaps, anxious that his followers, Gehazi-like, will try to turn his strange powers into a get-rich-quick stunt?

In any case, Jesus is determined to provide multi-dimensional healing. A leper could only be reintegrated into the community if given a clean bill of health by the local priest, not if he simply claimed to have been cured by a wandering preacher. But the ex-leper has no inhibitions: he tells people everywhere what has happened to him. Mark's strange story moves on, with the Galilean villagers discovering more of God's healing and grace than Herod, up the road in his palace, had ever dreamed of. Some things don't change.

Proper 3

—— ❧ ——

Isaiah 43.18–25
2 Corinthians 1.18–22
Mark 2.1–12

Forgiveness is always shocking, even when it's God who's doing it. Indeed, that's often the worst: in a paradox whose only solution is the depth of human pride, we shrink from the undeserved, and hence humbling, grace and love of God. We remain paralysed, locked within the cycles of our own folly.

Watch how it works. 'Look at my new creation!' says God, 'Look at the oases appearing in the desert!' 'How boring', say God's people, not even troubling to pray, let alone offer sacrifice; 'how pointless it all is.' We sometimes think of people battering heaven with cries for forgiveness, pleading with God to hear and be gracious. Isaiah's picture is of God battering earth with offers of forgiveness, pleading with his people to accept what is lavishly offered.

This gives extra depth to the story of Jesus' ruined roof. I assume, by the way, that the house whose roof was torn up for the paralysed man to be let down was Jesus' own: Mark says 'it was reported that he was at home', and it looks as though he had no chance to move anywhere else before the crowds pressed in. Thus, at the first level, Jesus' offer of forgiveness may have carried a wryly humorous meaning: 'Don't worry about the roof; your sins are forgiven!' But something in the tone of voice, perhaps, alerted hearers to the second level of meaning, the one regularly noticed. Jesus was aware that the man's problem was more than physical, and that to address the deeper level, of unresolved guilt and the crippling self-hatred that accrues from it, would be the way to address the obvious symptoms too.

What Isaiah's passage adds to the picture is the possibility that the bystanders' anger at Jesus' offer of forgiveness, though expressed in terms of theological orthodoxy, may itself have been an outward symptom of a deeper problem. Granted that humans in general, and even God's own people, find divine forgiveness so shocking, is it any wonder that it comes as an affront to find forgiveness standing there in human form, reaching out a hand, speaking words that functioned at several levels simultaneously? Is it not actually offensive that all God's promises find their 'Yes' in Jesus? Would we not find it easier to cope if things were more oblique?

The Corinthians were ready with their accusations, too. Paul, they say, is just muddling along, can't make up his mind whether he's coming or going. But (as the succeeding passage makes clear) Paul has had one consistent motive throughout: the love of the apostle for a wayward community, and the constant desire to let that love work appropriately in relation to a changing situation. It is the Corinthians that have vacillated in their allegiance to him, not he in his care for them. Jesus Christ, himself misunderstood precisely when freely offering love, stands at the heart of the unscrambling of the tangled relationship, facilitating God's work of establishing, anointing, sealing and promising.

The Second Sunday Before Lent

—— ∾ ——

Proverbs 8.1, 22–31
Colossians 1.15–20
John 1.1–14

Eyebrows will be raised at the reappearance of John's prologue so soon after Christmas. But our surprise at the lectionary's turns and twists is nothing to that launched upon the world by John's famous first 14 verses (better, his first 17 verses). Put them alongside Colossians 1, and you have some of the most explosive new thinking the Jewish traditions ever produced.

Let's be clear: this apparent novelty emerged within Judaism. It was not an alien import. Speaking of Jesus as the unique personal revelation of the one true God, as the one through whom the Creator made all things, was at one level a shock. Yet, both Colossians and John insist, it might have been guessed all along.

They both go back to Genesis: 'In the beginning, God created ... and made humans in his own image'. Jesus is the truly human one because he is himself the Image. But they also have Proverbs 8 in mind. Wisdom was YHWH's hand-maid, his personal agent, in the creation of the world, the one through whom all things were made. YHWH 'possessed' or 'begat' Wisdom before all things; YHWH was never without Wisdom. Thus, if humans want to reflect God's image in their daily life, Wisdom is what they need; the down-to-earth character of Proverbs corresponds precisely to the down-to-

34

earthness of the incarnation. The attentive reader of Proverbs is one in whom God's word becomes flesh on a daily basis.

Colossians, in particular, exploits the multiple possibilities of Proverbs 8.22 ('YHWH possessed me, the beginning') and Genesis 1.1 ('In the beginning, God created'). The Hebrew word for 'beginning' also means 'sum total', 'head', and 'firstfruits'; the word for 'in' can also mean 'through' and 'for'. The poem exploits these meanings within a simple structure. Christ is the one in, through and for whom creation (vv. 15–16) and redemption (vv. 18b–20) are accomplished; he is the start, the sum total, the head (vv. 17–18a). At one level this is a way of exulting in the wild glory of the incarnation and the hidden depths of God's word. At another, it prepares the ground for the practical teaching to come. Colossians is a true heir of the Jewish Wisdom tradition: celebrating the limitless splendour of God's creative and redemptive character and person, and living with both feet firmly on the ground. If God is precisely the *creator*, what else should we expect?

John has the same picture but within a simple and breathtaking storyline. New creation appears as God's gift within the first creation. The Word becomes flesh to reveal God's redemptive glory where it is desperately needed. The twist in the tale for us must always be: how are these words to become flesh, how is this God to be known at ground level, in today's world and Church? Unless we address that, Lady Wisdom has made her appeal in vain. And if the answer raises a few eyebrows, so be it.

The Sunday Next Before Lent

—— ∼ ——

2 Kings 2.1–12
2 Corinthians 4.3–6
Mark 9.2–9

Mark sees the Transfiguration as an anticipated fulfilment of the promise in the previous verse ('Some here will not die until they see the kingdom of God come with power'). The thin curtain separating God's dimension from ordinary life is pulled back, and mortals gaze on abiding heavenly realities. The coming of God's kingdom will involve earthly events; but those events will be precisely moments of revelation, unveiling God's power and presence.

Past and future telescope together into a dazzling present. Elijah and Moses (that way round, oddly, in Mark's account, highlighting Elijah as the forerunner and thus Jesus as the Coming One) stand for Prophets and Law, the context within which Jesus' work makes sense. Both had met God on the mountain, Moses in earthquake, wind and fire, Elijah in a still small voice. Which was this more like?

Peter blurts out a garbled suggestion designed to freeze the frame, to stop the moment in its tracks – the same futile instinct that makes us photograph a sunset. Then come the cloud and the voice, a Presence above and beyond that of the great heroes of old. The words confirm what was said at Jesus' baptism, assuring the terrified watchers that Jesus is indeed Messiah, and that his summons to follow must be obeyed.

These are the foothills of the event itself, which historians of Jesus often skirt round with embarrassment. It isn't a misplaced resurrection story, as used to be said: in the Easter narratives themselves, Jesus does not shine. It isn't the kind of story that first-century Jews would make up to express, 'mythologically', some aspect of their faith. It belongs, rather, with many accounts ancient and modern of the physical transformation that sometimes accompanies the sudden special and overpowering presence of the always-present God. When that happens, bodies may quiver and faces shine.

Such moments, unbidden and unpredictable, come not for their own sake but in relation to particular tasks. One day, after we had trudged for hours through freezing cloud in the Cairngorms, the clouds rolled back and we saw, for a few seconds, the path we had trodden and the crags that lay ahead. That spine-tingling combination of revelation and vocation was what the early Christians spoke of when, like Paul, they looked into the face of Jesus and there discovered not only the glory of God but also their own calling.

There has never been an easy time to be a Christian. It isn't only our own world that screams at us how futile and silly it is to believe in Jesus, let alone to follow him. Those who walk around in the fog, never glimpsing the sky or the path, claim that both are just wishful thinking, that nobody sees these things clearly anyway. But those who have seen the glory can never be the same again. Like Elisha with Elijah, we will not now leave this man until we have been assured of a share in his spirit.

Lent

The First Sunday of Lent

—— ∾ ——

Genesis 9.8–17
1 Peter 3.18–22
Mark 1.9–15

Noah is conspicuously absent from much of the New Testament. When he does appear, as in 1 Peter 3, it isn't immediately obvious why. Who were those 'spirits in prison' from Noah's day? In what sense did Jesus preach to them? How can Noah's ark help us understand baptism (apart from the obvious sense of coming through water to salvation)? And how does all this relate to what Peter is saying?

He is explaining why it is better to suffer for doing right than for doing wrong. Jesus' innocent suffering, as elsewhere in the letter, is the model for that of Christians. And those who, through Jesus' death and resurrection, belong to the one true God are assured that, since Jesus is already sovereign over all spiritual and temporal powers, they must not be afraid of what those powers can do to them. Standing before God with a clear conscience (vv. 16, 21), they know that whatever 'flesh' can do to them God's Spirit is stronger. (In v. 18 '*in* the flesh' and '*in* the Spirit' are better rendered 'by': Jesus was killed *by* mere mortals, and raised *by* God's Spirit.) Verses 18 and 22 set the parameters for the dense passage in between.

Christians stand before God on the basis of the fact and meaning of baptism. Coming through the water, with its

40

echoes of the creation narrative, the Noah story, and above all the Exodus, now receives yet more colouring from Jesus' representative dying and rising. Baptism symbolizes passing through tribulations, of which death is the greatest, to stand in the presence of the true sovereign one – as opposed to the petty tyrants who rant and rage against the subversive gospel.

Why Noah, then? Partly because he symbolizes God's grace, saving his people through terrible catastrophe. But also because that catastrophe came about, in the story, not least because of the wicked angels of Genesis 6.2. To them, and their equivalents in the first century, Jesus has already made the decisive proclamation: their rule, based on the power of sin and death, is broken. (This announcement is not, then, the same as that in 4.6, which seems to be to pre-Christian members of God's people.) Victory is won; the temporal and even spiritual powers ranged against the Church are a beaten rabble. The story of Noah is a vivid reminder, through the symbol of baptism, of who the Christian really is, and before whom he or she stands.

If this lesson, and this way of putting it, seem remote to comfortable Western Christians, whose fault is that? We do well to ponder the anguish of fellow Christians for whom tribunals, injustice and innocent suffering are daily realities. As we hear the Gospel story of Jesus' baptism, wilderness testing, and kingdom-announcement, we may ask ourselves, as a conscience-clearing exercise, not only which contemporary Christians are closest to the dominical pattern, but also which principalities and powers have tricked us into compromise and collusion.

The Second Sunday of Lent

——— ⟿ ———

Genesis 17.1–7, 15–16
Romans 4.13–25
Mark 8.31–38

Abraham and Peter offer a stark and sobering contrast. Abraham looks at his good-as-dead body and believes God's promise of life. Peter looks at his dreams of being the King's right-hand man and refuses to hear the King speaking of the royal vocation to suffer and die. Example and warning keep us on the Lenten path.

Abraham's faith is the badge, Paul insists, of his whole world-wide family. People still sometimes think that Paul left the Old Testament behind; nothing could be further from the truth. His gospel is all about the way in which Abraham's God has at last kept his promises. He has done so, however, in a startling fashion. Some translations bracket the end of verse 16 and the start of verse 17, but Abraham's being 'the father of many nations' and hence the father of all who believe, from whatever ethnic background, is part of the chapter's main theme and thrust. Part of Paul's point about faith is that it is open to all, not just those who possess the Jewish law as their ancestral code or circumcision as their covenant sign.

Behind this point, as so often in Romans, stands Paul's picture of God, the creator, the covenant-keeper: God gives life to the dead and calls non-existent things into being (v. 17). Even so, Paul seems to be saying, God can revive that Jewish covenant membership that was under sentence of death for its failure to keep the law (v. 15), and can also call as covenant members those who were outside the covenant by birth and inclination – in other words, Gentiles. The covenantal faithfulness of the creator God: that is what is unveiled in the gospel of Jesus.

But how does that gospel relate specifically to Abraham's faith? Here is Paul's master-stroke. Abraham looked at God's promises, recognized that they meant that God would give life where there was none, and believed. The Christian listens to the gospel message that the creator God raised the Messiah from the dead, recognizes that this means God doing what is normally impossible, and believes. Faith here is not so much 'in' this or that event (still less is it 'a general religious attitude to life'), but active and personal trust in the God who characteristically acts in this way.

It was this faith that Peter sadly lacked, looking at things from a human point of view, not God's. He could not see that the way to life was the way of the cross. He was, like the rest of them, looking for Israel's redemption. But he had not yet penetrated to the secret at the heart of Israel's vocation: that Israel's God, the world's creator, took delight in acting in this topsy-turvy fashion, precisely to redeem a topsy-turvy world – and called his followers to do the same. To be ashamed of this God, to refuse this path, is not just cowardice. It is to miss the point altogether.

The Third Sunday of Lent

—— ∿ ——

Exodus 20.1–17
1 Corinthians 1.18–25
John 2.13–22

Jewish jokes testify to the terror of the Ten Words from Sinai. Headache? Do what Moses did: take two tablets. Moses to the people: we've got them down from twenty to ten, but adultery is still in. Moses to God: How much do these tablets cost? God: They're free. Moses: Fine, I'll have two.

Irreverent? No; rather the reflex of reverence, the nervous need for safe space between us and God. The Commandments are spoken, not intimately to Moses, but in thunder and trumpet, audible for miles around. People who advocate getting back to the Commandments (not that they normally want a prohibition of all images, or a seventh-day sabbath) don't usually envisage the earthquake, wind and fire of Sinai.

The Ten Words were God's way of life for God's redeemed people, the covenant charter between YHWH and Israel. The two tablets most likely each contained all the commandments: one complete document for each party. So why did Moses retain both? Because, as Exodus continues, God also commanded appropriate provision for his own presence to accompany the people. Only when we grasp Israel's dread before the mountain will we understand why the tabernacle, too, was threatening. And why, when Moses delayed on the mountain, a darker perversion of reverence came into play: the creation of safer, less demanding gods,

44

cheap parodies of the God whose only appropriate image is loving, breathing human life.

Law and tabernacle were not themselves images of God. They were signposts, pointing to the God who speaks, who is mysteriously present, who has redeemed and will now guide. This utter demand, and dread presence, are the hallmarks, too, of the gospel Paul preached: the message of the crucified Messiah, the redeeming yet all-demanding message of the God who had come as a living, loving, self-giving human being and had embodied that strange presence to the uttermost.

Human fear invents jokes, human wisdom invents systems, to keep this God at bay. The message of Calvary pierces through, working its healing yet wounding way from the heart of the living God to the heart of human need. The Lenten journey to the foot of that other terrible mountain must renounce the signs, the wisdom, the idolatry and perhaps even the humour that domesticate what we find there. Otherwise (God forgive us) we will first trivialize the truth and then denounce it for its triviality.

If Jesus embodies yet transcends the deepest meaning of the law – God's truly human way of life – he also embodies and transcends the tabernacle and its successor, the Temple. His outburst against its abuse, and his coded message about destruction and rebuilding, are the reactions of truth to parody. They form for us a final challenge: whatever downgrades or domesticates the full revelation of the living God must be set aside. Nothing and no one but the crucified and risen Jesus, terrible as Sinai, mysterious as the tabernacle, must be both our goal and our guide through the wilderness.

The Fourth Sunday of Lent

—— ∾ ——

Numbers 21.4–9
Ephesians 2.1–10
John 3.14–21

The serpent slithers its way through myth and legend, poetry and art. Too potent a symbol to be ignored, some cultures have worshipped it, while others have feared and loathed it. Freud said predictable things about it, echoed in D. H. Lawrence's famous poem and in numerous pop-psychology theories about getting in touch with our darker sides.

To the surprise of some brought up on Numbers 21 and John 3, where the bronze serpent on the pole foreshadows Jesus on the cross, the image of a snake twined around a staff had long been a symbol of healing, perhaps of the healing god himself, in (for instance) the cult of Asclepius. And the serpent who makes his first entrance in the third chapter of the Bible remains at least a background figure until he receives his final doom in the third chapter from the end. The serpent embodies or reflects human beliefs about our deep disease and its ultimate cure.

Jewish and Christian traditions frame this symbol within their historical stories of creation and redemption. Mark's extra ending envisages Christians handling snakes. In Acts, Paul survives a deadly snakebite. Mary, in some icons, tramples on the serpent; in some paintings she teaches the boy Jesus to do so. Here Moses' bronze serpent shines a startling light on the cross.

The serpent is hardly an image of Jesus, despite the surface parallel. That which was poisoning the people is displayed as a beaten foe, just as for John evil itself is judged, condemned and defeated on the cross. The Lenten gaze on the ugly gallows at the crossroads of history is the look that brings life.

Redemption is, after all, not a matter of taming or befriending the serpent, but of defeating it and of creation thereby emerging into light out of old darkness. The strange divine love, of which the too-famous John 3.16 speaks, is not the laissez-faire tolerance that accepts everything and everybody the way they are. It is the potent and tenacious transforming energy that deals with the darkness, that defeats the rulers of the world, that banishes the serpent at last, and creates – not a new garden, with a reptile house to keep the serpent alive but harmless! – but the city of God where all is light, and where, as on certain islands that pride themselves on the fact, serpents are banished for good.

The Christian gospel, classically stated in Ephesians 2, speaks not of Yin and Yang, but of sin and forgiveness, of evil power and victorious divine mercy, of the passions of the flesh and the new bodily life in Christ. This is not dualistic. There is such a thing as Evil, and it is not the necessary other side of Good. There is such a thing as mercy, and mercy does not relabel or redescribe 'evil' as 'good'. I do not know, and I do not think anybody knows, why there was a serpent in the garden; but that there will be none in the city I have no doubt.

The Fifth Sunday of Lent
(Passiontide begins)

—— ∽ ——

Jeremiah 31.31–34
Hebrews 5.5–10
John 12.20–33

Imagine the simple request echoing along the corridors of church bureaucracy. It is passed from office to office, from secretary to secretary. It is left on voice-mails and e-mails, faxed through to headquarters, scribbled in shorthand for later typed memos. They phone the biblical studies departments, but they are busy with the Christology of Q and the pseudonymity of Ephesians. They call the history departments, but they have stopped talking about people and events and now explore the social construction of fictive narratival worlds. And the Greeks at the feast, then and now, wait patiently with their request: Sir, we wish to see Jesus.

Is there anyone else to see, anything else to ask for? So simple a question as to be touchingly naive (like the Salvation Army lassie asking the bishop if he's saved), or possibly cloyingly manipulative: in synods, when somebody says people should stop listening to each other and start listening to Jesus, it usually turns out that on this question Jesus and the speaker happen to agree. But that doesn't mean we shouldn't be stopped in our tracks, in the middle of Lent of all times, and confronted with the question: what about Jesus? Can we please get to see him? Here's a bracing pre-

Holy Week question, for individuals and church structures: to what extent does what we do contribute to an answer?

Having said all that, we note that John does not have Jesus hurrying off to meet these enquiring foreigners. Instead, he regards their question as a further sign that the hour is coming at which, through his apparently tragic death, he will bear much fruit. Through his 'lifting up' he will draw all people to himself. The rulers of the world, human and superhuman, are to be put down. People of all sorts are to come and worship the true king.

The request to see Jesus may of course be expressed inarticulately or obliquely. We have to learn to hear it within the symbols of a culture as well as in face-to-face questions. But only when we are answering the request, paradoxically, can we see the relevance of Hebrews's exploration of Jesus as the great High Priest, which initially seems hardly the place to start a simple answer. By bringing together Psalms 2 and 110 (both common early christological texts) the author portrays Jesus as that strange double combination, a king who is also a priest, the unique Son of God who suffered, wept and died as a fully human being.

Find ways of saying that without technical language: explore ways of talking about politics and religion which converge on Jesus, discover language about divinity and humanity which, instead of competing, complement each other at the point of Jesus; and you will be well on the way to showing Jesus to the Greeks at today's feast. 'They shall all know me,' says God through Jeremiah, promising covenant renewal. If that's true, why can't we answer the question?

Palm Sunday
(Liturgy of the Passion)

—— ∽ ——

Isaiah 50.4–9a
Philippians 2.5–11
Mark 14.1—15.47

'In spite of that, we call this Friday good.' They didn't at the time, but Jesus' surprised friends, and some very surprised enemies, quickly found themselves telling the horrid and brutal tale as the story of God's unthinkable salvation.

Within three decades Paul condensed into 36 Greek words what it would take Mark 119 verses to narrate. 'In God's form, but not thinking to exploit equality with God, he emptied himself, taking a servant's form, born in human likeness; found in human form, humble and obedient unto death, the death of the cross.' Hidden there are five lenses through which to view the story, and Paul puts two more at the head. One for each day of Holy Week, perhaps.

First, Jesus' own human story. The leader weeping alone in the garden. The truth-teller mocked as a false prophet. The peace-bringer arraigned as a rebel. The God-forsaken man of God. Saving meaning is not superimposed upon this human story, but discovered within it.

Second, the story of Adam, primal humanity, all-of-us in mythic perspective. Humans in God's image, snatching at equality with God, becoming servants of sin and death. The human story of arrogance, greed and tragic consequences.

Inside Mark's story, listen to the cry of crippled human-kind.

Third, the story of Israel, the Lord's servant. Israel enslaved in Egypt, burdened and groaning. Israel exiled, songless in a strange land. Israel persecuted, mocked by the nations, polluted, overrun, ruled by traitors and oppressors, clinging to God's promise of vindication even as the back is beaten and the beard pulled out. The redeeming people themselves in need of servant-redemption. Read Mark as the story of Israel's vocation uniquely fulfilled.

Fourth, the Emperor. Caesar (so said Roman flattery) was equal to God, had been a servant of the state, and was now exalted. Paul and Mark alike point to the strange enthrone-ment of the world's true monarch – and, thereby, to the redefinition of monarchy itself.

Fifth, God's own story. Consider at every step along this verbal Via Dolorosa: this figure is the incarnate one. Forget the shallow idea that he stopped being God in order to become human, to suffer and die. The gospel message is precisely that this beaten, broken and bedraggled creature ('some of you', as the newsreaders say, 'may find this picture distressing' – and there's something wrong if we don't) was indeed God's Son, the living presence of the God we thought we knew but perhaps didn't, or not well enough.

Enough there already, you may think. But Paul adds: this is the way you should think among yourselves. Identify by all means with the minor characters in the story, but identify, corporately, with Christ himself. The suffering Church follows in the steps of the Master.

And finally, of course, we are each to walk this way alone. Mark 14 and 15 stand under the rubric of Mark 8.34, where the subject is singular: to follow, take up the cross.

Easter

Easter Day

—— ∾ ——

Isaiah 25.6–9
1 Corinthians 15.1–11
John 20.1–18

This Gospel reading is not, as one writer has suggested, 'a sanitized story about a trip to a garden and a lovely surprise'. If Easter is in any sense the happy ending after a sad story, that is the least important thing about it. It is not primarily an ending, but a beginning. It is the start of God's new creation.

Line up John 20 alongside John's prologue (1.1–18). The themes come full circle: light and darkness, new life 'in' the Word, the right of Jesus' followers to become children of God (in v. 17, for the first time, Jesus calls God '*your* Father ... and *your* God'). The later scene with Thomas echoes 1.18: the Son has unveiled the invisible God. John 1 echoes Genesis 1; in John 20, God's new day has dawned. Twice John reminds us that it is the first day of the week.

Of all the passages which strike me as eyewitness testimony from the shadowy figure we call 'the beloved disciple', verse 8 is among the strongest. This 'other disciple', who had reached the tomb first but had paused and allowed Peter to go in ahead, went in, 'and he saw – *and believed*'. Simple words with limitless depth.

This is a moment of great intimacy and power. As many find when they hear this story, the previously unthinkable dawns, not as the logical conclusion of an argument, nor as a scientific proof, but as a sudden but lasting warmth of heart and mind, an assurance in whose light the rest of the world makes a different and more powerful sort of sense. Don't be fooled by the way people talk of 'belief' as a lesser kind of 'knowledge' ('Is it raining?' 'I believe so' – in other words, I don't know for sure); when John says 'he saw and believed' he is talking at the level of world-view, speaking of rock-bottom convictions that create the context within which knowledge itself can spring to new life.

This new sort of believing is hardly, then, the recognition that Jesus had simply 'gone to heaven' – as one frequently hears people say, both outside the Church and inside. As Paul emphasized, quoting the earliest known confession of Christian faith, this was an event that happened at a specific time after the crucifixion (if Jesus had 'gone to heaven when he died', why would anyone suppose it had taken place 'on the third day'?).

Jews like John and Paul believed firmly that the souls of God's people were in God's hand against the day when, in the future, God would raise them all to new life. If all Easter had done was to reaffirm that belief, there would have been no news, no new creation, no reason to break into a trot, let alone a breathless chase (people hardly ever run in the Gospels; on Easter morning they do little else). Isaiah spoke of death being abolished. Beware of speaking, instead, of its being merely redescribed.

The Second Sunday of Easter

———— ∾ ————

Acts 4.32–35
1 John 1.1—2.2
John 20.19–31

'Peace be with you', said Jesus. And again, two verses later, 'Peace be with you.' Like a great bell, a single note with multiple overtones, the promise of peace tolls out across the world. Not just an inner peace of heart for every individual who hears and believes. Not just an agenda for peace for a warring world. The old Hebrew word *Shalom* speaks of a quality of life which includes but transcends both: rich and fruitful human living, God's new creation bursting into many-coloured flower.

The peace declaration is flanked with simple but profound actions. Jesus shows the disciples his hands and his side, the marks of the love which had loved them to the uttermost, the signs that the bill had been paid (compare 19.30, where 'It is finished' means, among other things, 'the price is paid'). Easter means, amidst much else, that peace, never other than costly, has truly been purchased on the cross.

As often in John, we move quickly from love's evidence to love's commission. New creation again: Jesus breathes on the disciples, as God breathed on the first human pair, to make them living beings of a new sort, peace-bringers, sin-forgivers. 'As the Father sent me, so I send you': the highest possible ecclesiology, grounded in the highest possible Christology, made effective by the gift of the Spirit. Peace is not so

56

much a state of being, more a power let loose upon the world.

For Thomas, peace comes in person to confront the warring spirits of doubt. Scepticism was not born in the eighteenth century; believing in Jesus' resurrection is not a matter of the ancient world struggling to convince the modern one, but of the creator's power confronting the age-old assumption of all humankind – the potter, you might say, confronting the clay. But if Easter peace brings order to the world's confusion, it also brings glorious confusion to the world's order, opening up undreamed-of possibilities, not so much of random miracles but of new creation in place of decay, new peace in place of war.

The Church perceived very quickly what this might mean. To sell ancestral property and share the proceeds was not a matter of primitive communism. It was a renunciation of one of the central Jewish symbols. It went alongside the rejection of the Temple as the centre, the Torah as the defining charter, and Jewish ethnicity as the necessary qualification, of God's people. Jesus and the Spirit took the place of all, in a new symbolic universe appropriate for the new covenant and the new creation.

Barnabas's sale of a field was as important, symbolically, as Jeremiah's buying of one (Jeremiah 32). It was a sign of that fellowship, that partnership (*koinonia*, another great bell-like word), of which John's first letter speaks, again with disarming and deceptive simplicity. Life, light, fellowship, forgiveness: these, among many others, make up the overtones that give the great bell of *Shalom* its particular note.

The Third Sunday of Easter

—— ∾ ——

Acts 3.12–19
1 John 3.1–7
Luke 24.36–48

The ancient world knew all about ghosts, visions, apparitions, and spooks. Ancient literature has plenty of people being found alive after being supposed dead, plenty of spirits of the dead returning to haunt, spy on, or chat with the living. Jesus' disciples could easily have used such categories to explain their extraordinary experiences of the presence of the risen Jesus.

That they did not is powerful testimony to what actually happened. People sometimes suggest that Luke and John, writing late in the first century (so it is supposed; the evidence for this is not as strong as sometimes imagined), were at pains to make Jesus' resurrection appearances more 'physical' than they had actually been, to combat the view that Jesus wasn't truly human, but only 'seemed' to be (the heresy known as 'Docetism'). Frankly, if that was what Luke was trying to do he made a very botched job of it. For Jesus to be touched, and to eat broiled fish, is one thing. Appearing through locked doors, disappearing after breaking bread at Emmaus, and finally withdrawing into God's heavenly dimension – none of this strikes one as immediately useful in a fight against Docetism.

The real explanation is stranger, and is backed up by evidence of various kinds. The disciples were confronted

58

with a new form of reality, for which they were unprepared, but for which the language of resurrection (not of ghosts, or of mere resuscitations) was available. Jesus, they believed, had gone through death and out the other side into a new mode of life. This was, naturally enough, difficult to describe, but it seems to have involved his physical body being transformed so that it was now inhabiting both our space and God's space.

This new mode of being is regarded, in the New Testament, as both the model for the future of Christians and the source of power for life in the present. There aren't words to describe what we shall be, says John, but when Jesus is revealed we shall be like him. We shall see him as he is; since you become like what you worship, we shall thus be changed into his likeness, into the Easter mode of being. Mind-boggling, of course, but that's the point. Good theology requires good imagination.

Easter humanity, in fact, is genuine humanity, as opposed to humanity distorted and defaced by sin, decay and death. One of the great lies of our time is that abstaining from sin means failure to live a fully human life. Resurrection power comes to us, as it were, from our future, so that we can anticipate the truly human life in the here and now. When John says 'no one who abides in him sins' the tense of the latter verb is continuous: sin, though still a possibility, is not now our continual, habitual situation and state. The power that healed the physical cripple, glorifying the God of Israel in the process, is available to heal moral cripples as well.

The Fourth Sunday of Easter

—— ∼ ——

Acts 4.5–12
1 John 3.16–24
John 10.11–18

The text about the rejected stone has itself become something of a stumbling stone. The point of the quotation from Psalm 118.22 is that, though Jesus appeared to the 'builders' of Judaism (the Chief Priests in particular) to be unusable, God had other ideas. The unique shape that made the stone useless for their building qualified it exactly to be the cornerstone, or keystone, of God's building. One stone and only one of that shape was needed: Jesus is it.

Thus, as the next verse explains, 'there is salvation in no one else'. No other name will do; if it's salvation you want, it's Jesus or nothing. What arrogance, shrieks the relativist. This is Christian imperialism, sniffs the secularist. Many paths up the same mountain, murmurs the sophisticate. This is now becoming a fashionable argument against the bodily resurrection of Jesus: it commits us, people say, to a politically incorrect view of 'other religions'. It means that Christianity possesses a truth that the others do not. Back comes the answer from the early Christians: only one resurrection; only one Jesus.

Now of course 'Christianity' covers not just the opening affirmation but two thousand years of faith and folly, wisdom and wickedness. However, just because the Inquisition happened, just because the Constantinian settlement

60

was ambiguous, that doesn't mean the resurrection wasn't unique, or that there are lots of different paths to salvation. There is such a thing as Christian imperialism, and may God save us from it; but the abuse of truth shouldn't impugn the truth itself.

The entire New Testament speaks of a saving act which stands out from all others. No other name speaks of innocent life laid down for others, generating spontaneous love for the outsider and the needy. One of the reasons Christianity spread in the Roman world was that nobody had ever looked after the sick and friendless with the self-sacrificial love that the Christians showed. This name speaks of love with skin on, then and now.

It speaks, too, not of an abstract religious experience, of a general sense of 'the divine', but of the personal mutual knowing of shepherd and sheep. There are such persons as hired hands who don't care for the sheep; there are such creatures as wolves. When it comes to religion, we do not live in a vacuum, where all explorations are equally safe and successful, and where there are no dangers and pitfalls. It's a jungle out there, and the sheep need a shepherd. No other shepherd lays down his life on behalf of the sheep, and then takes it again.

It was of course politically incorrect – indeed, disastrously foolish – for Peter and the others to say all this before the Jewish authorities. But the healing miracle on a lifelong cripple was undeniable, and they claimed it had come about through the powerful name of the risen Jesus. Healing power and powerful love are the signs which enable the Church to speak the truth about Jesus.

The Fifth Sunday of Easter

—— ❧ ——

Acts 8.26–40
1 John 4.7–21
John 15.1–8

If you like evangelism, you'll love Philip's story. A spirit-led meeting with a court official, who happens to be reading Isaiah 53 and asking the right questions. There is time to converse at leisure; there is water for baptism when required and requested.

The Ethiopian eunuch was a gentile God-fearer. He couldn't have been a proselyte; as a eunuch he was disqualified anyway, and since many eunuchs were partially dismembered as well as castrated he couldn't be circumcised. You probably didn't want to know that; some people might read this piece straight after breakfast. But you won't understand the story without it.

This black man (there was, by the way, remarkably little colour prejudice in the ancient world) had been to Jerusalem to worship Israel's God, *and he wouldn't have been allowed to celebrate the festival*. Physically unfit, ritually excluded; all that way and no entrance ticket when he arrived. He could have prayed at a distance, but that was it. And yet Israel's God still so captivates him that he's reading Isaiah on the way home. Was there something in chapter 53 that caught his eye? 'In his humiliation, justice was denied him.' I wonder.

There were two traditions of reading Isaiah 53 at the time. One saw the servant as the Messiah, but the sufferings were

62

what he inflicted on the pagans. The other saw the servant as the righteous martyrs, but they weren't Messiahs. Philip puts them together, and embodies the result, announcing to this black eunuch that in Jesus Israel's God has revealed his universal welcome, and showing him by his own welcome what that servant-love looks like. Suddenly the Ethiopian's physical, social and cultic exclusion is overturned. He is embraced by the God who is revealed in the crucified Jesus, and welcomed gladly by the evangelist who represents his master. And (of course) he goes on his way rejoicing.

Result: a new branch is added to the vine, 'made clean', as Jesus says, 'by the word that has been spoken to you'. The vine was a symbol of Israel, pruned and kept pure by the God-given cult and its symbolic world. But if the crucified and risen Jesus is now the true vine, the new symbols – the empty cross, the empty tomb – speak of a different sort of cleansing, a dealing with sin and death (two of the main pollutants in the Temple system) once and for all, a free welcome of overflowing love for all who hear and receive. New branch, new life, new responsibilities, new power. If the Ethiopian Church is to be believed, the eunuch went home and bore fruit that lasts to this day.

John's letter weaves a Trinitarian pattern in honour of this overflowing divine love. That's how much God loves, he says; and that's how much we should love one another. In the New Testament, 'love' regularly describes not so much how people feel as what they do. What might that look like? Step forward, Philip.

The Sixth Sunday of Easter

—— ∾ ——

Acts 10.44–48
1 John 5.1–6
John 15.9–17

'His commandments are not burdensome.' Hard to take, that, in a world where *all* commandments are burdensome, where anybody telling anyone else what to do – even God telling his creatures what to do – is felt as an imposition, a belittling or patronizing attempt to keep people down.

But John, let alone Jesus, won't let us get away with that. Loving God means keeping his commandments; and the greatest commandment is love. Circular? Maybe, but not viciously so. The upward widening spiral of Christian commitment uproots us from the swampy ground of the romantic movement, where everything that is not generated by our own 'feelings' is somehow 'inauthentic', and replants us in the firm soil of God's conquest of 'the world'. This is where the vine can grow best, and where its branches can bear fruit that will last. This is where prayer to the Father in the name of the Son will surely be answered.

But what does it mean to pray in the name of the Son? Jesus Christ came 'not with water only, but with water and blood'. He was not, that is, simply a human being who had become 'divine' at his baptism, but was the full Son of God, supremely in his death. Even so, those who believe this complete gospel are to be marked not by a super-spirituality which will take them out of the real world, but by a Jesusspirituality in which moral effort and world-conquest go hand in hand. 'His yoke is easy and his burden light'; yes, but that doesn't mean that yokes and burdens are themselves a bad thing. In that context (read on a little in John 15 and you'll see how relevant it is) specific prayer is neither selfish nor whimsical, but rather the expression of the life of God already flowing through the branches of the vine.

What matters, then, is the Spirit. Not a general religious feeling, or a sense of 'the spiritual' as opposed to 'the material', but the Spirit of Jesus, known by bearing witness to Jesus, recognized, as was the risen Jesus himself, through the marks of world-conquering suffering. The Spirit brings people into a partnership with Jesus, a friendship where commandments are neither arbitrarily imposed nor obeyed without comprehension, but are part of a shared strategy to which all are gladly signed up.

Conquest of the world is not a negative thing, like the Vietnam soldiers who claimed they had 'to destroy the village in order to save it'. It is a conquest of the present structures and power-systems of the world, through which humans are enslaved. In the early Church the most obvious of these was the sky-high wall that separated Jews from Gentiles. But when Peter preached at Cornelius's house, the Gentiles heard the gospel message, and found that, believing it, new languages of praise came naturally. The wall came tumbling down. Water and Spirit testified that the commandment of love was not burdensome.

The Seventh Sunday of Easter
(Sunday after Ascension Day)

——— ∼ ———

Acts 1.15–17, 21–26
1 John 5.9–13
John 17.6–19

The interesting thing about the choice of Matthias has
nothing to do with Matthias himself. Nor is it the striking
method of his selection, which if applied today would
simplify clergy appointments no end. It is the fact that it
was deemed necessary. The Twelve were one short.

Instead of regarding Judas's demise as the beginning of a
process of natural wastage – the Twelve did not appoint
further successors when, quite soon after this, they began to
be killed off – they saw it, on biblical grounds inconveniently
omitted by the squeamish lectionary, as constituting a hole
needing to be plugged. The symbolism of the twelve tribes
had to be maintained for the initial witness to make its point.
The prophets had foretold that Israel would be regathered;
most of the tribes, after all, had long since disappeared when
the northern kingdom was devastated seven hundred years
earlier. Even before the covenant-renewing wind and fire of
Pentecost, the young Church found its identity in the belief
that in Jesus these prophecies had come true.

Much of the New Testament's language about the Church
can be seen as filling in this belief. In the Johannine writings
this regularly means the combination of two things: the

Church's witness to, but separation from, the world, and the Church's inner or spiritual life, through which the startling claims it makes become true at every level of the person and the community.

The first of these involves a tough balancing act. 'In the world', we say, 'but not of the world', summing up John 17; and yet the smooth little steps by which 'in' turns into 'of' are the dance that comes naturally to our wayward feet. Conversely, when we see the danger, the strides by which 'not of' becomes 'not in' march us towards a dualism which makes nonsense of the incarnation itself, not to mention the ascension of the still-human Jesus. Israel, of course, wrestled with the same problem, oscillating between compromise and hostility. Both sides in today's Church can tell horror stories about the other, reinforcing either position by rejection of its polar opposite.

One might then say that the inner life of the Christian and the Church should steer us along a broad middle way between the two; but the reality is on a different plane, in which the strengths of both extremes are combined. The first letter of John speaks of having God's testimony deep within ourselves, evidenced by the core belief in the fully human Jesus as fully God's son. The high-priestly prayer of Jesus in John 17, whose texture is so rich that we may choke on it unless we chew it slowly, speaks of God's word spoken in Jesus, God's name revealed in Jesus, and God's glory given through Jesus. Together these constitute the disciples in their inner selves, despite their own muddles and mistakes, as God's holy people for God's needy world. Unless they are holy, they will do the world no good.

Day of Pentecost

— ∾ —

Acts 2.1–21
Romans 8.22–27
John 15.26–27; 16.4b–15

It is one of the striking features of the New Testament that Luke, Paul and John, so very different as writers and theologians, sing in rich harmony when it comes to the Spirit.

At the heart of the music is the sense of uncontainable newness. The sneering reaction on the day of Pentecost wasn't too silly: in a sense the disciples *were* filled with new wine, and the old wineskins were showing signs of splitting. Or, in Pauline language, the groaning of all creation was now located within the believers themselves, so that the tension between the old world and the new had become an inner tension within the Christian, longing for the resurrection body which would give appropriate physical expression to the astonishing new energy welling up within.

Or, in Johannine language, the Spirit demonstrates, in a quasi-judicial fashion (it isn't only Paul who uses legal metaphors), that the world is in the wrong. It's in the wrong in its modes of morality (the cardinal sin is not believing in Jesus); in its notion of justice (the world's justice sent Jesus to the cross, but God's justice uses that as the means of Jesus' glorification); and in its eager judgement (it condemned Jesus, but actually his death was the condemnation of 'the ruler of this world'). The Spirit makes God's people sing out of tune with the rebellious and

68

decaying world. Pentecost is, after all, the festival of the giving of the Law on Sinai, 50 days after the Exodus, marking out Israel as God's peculiar people.

But just when we might think that the Spirit was taking us out of the world altogether, making us a cult of flaky fanatics, the same writers make it clear that the Spirit is the agent of creation's renewal and redemption. This is the same Spirit that brooded over creation, that spoke through the prophets. John has Jesus breathe the Spirit into the disciples precisely at the resurrection, the moment when the old world is brought to new life after death. Paul envisages the whole created order as a woman going into the pains of labour, longing for the child to be born in which her destiny as a mother will be fulfilled. Luke, through Peter's fresh reading of Joel, indicates that this new experience will bring about the reconciliation of young and old, slave and free, male and female, heaven and earth.

Too idealistic? Don't settle for less than the ideal vision. But expect, in embracing it, to be called to groan in prayer. It isn't only the individual Christian, but the whole community, that needs the Spirit's help in our weakness. Precisely when we are confronted again, in our communities as well as in our selves, with the pains and problems of our continued un-redeemed existence – that is the time when the Christ-shaped dialogue of Spirit and Father, which is what Christian prayer is all about, can flourish. The harmony of Pentecost depends on precisely this paradox.

Ordinary Time

Trinity Sunday

— ⟣ —

Isaiah 6.1–8
Romans 8.12–17
John 3.1–17

God's love, Jesus' death, new life in the Spirit. The irreducible minimum Christian story; yet, like Julian of Norwich's small nut, this well rounded little truth contains all that there is.

Trinity Sunday, of course, celebrates not a new truth, something else beyond Pentecost, but rather what you see when the excitement and drama of Pentecost has made its mark and you pause to reflect on it all. Or, if you prefer, Trinity Sunday is where you find yourself when, having been swept off your feet by the rushing mighty wind, you get up, dust yourself down, and survey your new surroundings.

The room where you are now standing is filled with light and warmth. Sunlight streams in from open windows and skylights, bathing every corner in its glow. The room is large but curiously shaped, being long and quite thin, but with lateral extensions either side about two-thirds of the way along. Exploring, you discover that within this shape there is everything you need for a rich and fulfilling human life. And, as you make your way around, you realize something else. The air you are breathing has a different taste – like exchanging the city for the mountains, only more so. It's clearer and fresher, and you feel as though with that stuff in your lungs you could do things you'd only dreamed of up to now.

In the New Testament the Trinity isn't an abstract theory, it's where you live. And, hence, *how* you live; 'fulfilling' means also 'challenging'. Breathing this air, you find yourself not only discovering the otherwise distant or unknowable God as a loving, wise and very present father, but also being called to do something that might otherwise look suicidal. 'Putting to death the deeds of the body' seems a strange way of *avoiding* death, but that's the logic of the new Christ-shaped life: the layout of this room means that certain otherwise apparently desirable activities are ruled out. This, and nowhere else, is where true humanness (otherwise known as 'holiness') flourishes, and the delicious air helps us believe (which we otherwise mightn't) that this is so.

We wish it always felt like this. The layout of the room, though, prevents anyone seeing more than part of it at any one moment. We never have it in our power. 'Born of water and the Spirit': ah, says someone in one corner, then I share this room with all the baptized. No, says another, I share it with those who experience the Spirit the same way I do. Nicodemus would like to have explained the new room in terms of the old, but he couldn't. Isaiah was overcome with guilt, individual and corporate, at seeing the unseeable thrice-holy God. (Repeating an adjective three times is a Hebrew form of superlative; as George MacLeod used to say, 'if you think that's a coincidence, I wish you a very dull life'.) Holiness goes with humility. It is, after all, God's room, not ours.

Proper 4

—— ∾ ——

1 Samuel 3.1–10
2 Corinthians 4.5–12
Mark 2.23—3.6

Like a cathedral chorister, Samuel has been brought to live and work in the atmosphere of prayer, worship and pilgrimage. Considering the lively human interest, it's surprising this story didn't entice the great classical artists; there is one painting of it, by the seventeenth-century Gerbrand van den Eekhout, in the Ashmolean Museum in Oxford.

As so often in biblical 'call' narratives (Ezekiel 1, Isaiah 6, Revelation 1), there is a darker side; again as usual, the lectionary misses it out. The previous chapter introduced Hophni and Phinehas, the sons of the ageing priest Eli. Eli has been warned about their cynical corruption, but he seems incapable of putting things right. Now God chooses young Samuel, wide-eyed and eager, to declare the word of judgement. When he says 'Speak, your servant is listening,' what follows is enough to make him wish his parents had never brought him in the first place. Samuel has the unenviable task of telling his guardian the news of imminent judgement. His fearless later ministry was rooted in his earliest experiences of hearing, and then speaking, God's word.

You can omit the confrontational material in 1 Samuel if you try hard enough; but you can't do that with Mark, which from the start pits Jesus against powers and authorities, human and spiritual, actual and self-appointed. Mark's framing of these two sabbath-controversies shows what he thinks they're about. They aren't merely instances of 'legalism', with Jesus as the great teacher of a non-legal, or non-ritual, kind of religion. They are all about the new thing that is bursting into the world through his presence and authority, a new thing for which the best precedent was God's new action in and through King David (2.25–6; see 1 Samuel 21.1–9). At the time referred to, David had been already anointed by Samuel. Saul was still king, and David was on the run from him; but he still claimed the right to eat the holy bread, a sign perhaps of his coming kingdom. Jesus now claims the right to put into action his own kingdom-path which would make redundant the customs by which Israel guarded its national life. And, just as one of Saul's servants went and told his master (1 Samuel 21.7; 22.9–10), so the Pharisees got together with the Herodians – hardly their natural allies! – to conspire against Jesus. This incident is one of many in which the shadow of the cross falls across Mark's whole narrative.

Paul's apostolic vocation, like Samuel's prophetic one, was not meant to be comfortable. In fact, he saw his sufferings as part of the point: they were a sign of the message he had to speak. But those in whose hearts God has shone the light of his glory will, like both prophet and apostle, have no hesitation in saying what has to be said. It is not themselves that they speak of, after all, but the King, the Lord.

Proper 5

—— ~ ——

1 Samuel 8.4–11[12–15]16–20[11.14–15]
2 Corinthians 4.13—5.1
Mark 3.20–35

So: did God want Israel to have a king, or didn't he? The question haunts not only this passage in 1 Samuel but much of the rest of the account of the monarchy, from the ill-fated Saul right down to the exile. Of course, David himself, and then Solomon, are fêted and celebrated (albeit with devastating criticisms). Hezekiah and Josiah are seen, later, as models. But most of the kings lived up to Samuel's warnings, and more so. Verse 18 says it all: *your* king, whom *you* have chosen for yourself. It sounds like God's contemptuous words to Moses in Exodus 32.7.

This story sets up a tension which is only resolved in the person of Jesus, and then only in his royal, messianic death. The people wanted a king because they didn't want God himself to be their king; they wanted someone on to whom they could project their own idolatries and have him legitimate them (8.8). Nevertheless, God gave them a king; and, when he removed him, he raised up a man to whom he would make extraordinary promises, seen in the New Testament as fulfilled in Jesus himself (2 Samuel 7, Psalm 2, etc.; see e.g. Romans 1.3–4; 15.12). The early Christians believed that in Jesus the riddle of 1 Samuel 8.7–9 had been solved. Here at last was a human king who was owed the allegiance proper to the one true God. And he, though the true king, took upon himself the folly and shame of all those who went before, bearing in his own body the pains of a thousand years of misguided monarchy.

The same tension crackles through Mark 3 as Jesus' family think he's mad, his enemies think he's demon-possessed, and Jesus himself responds by redefining his family around himself. Mark 3.31–35 is stark to the point of rudeness. Jesus does not 'belong' to his own human family any more. He will not be seen in terms of them. He is pioneering God's new work, God's restored Israel, and its nucleus is not defined in terms of parentage, brothers and sisters by blood. It is defined in terms of God's will; and Jesus sweepingly assumes that doing God's will means sitting around him and hearing his teaching. This king won't steal people from Israel in order to lord it over them, as Samuel warned. This king will teach them the truth and so set them free.

The tension between the kingdom you can see and the one you can't echoes on in the promise of the resurrection body. Like Samuel's challenge to the Israelites, Paul's challenge to the Corinthians is to trust God for his kingdom, for the 'house' kept ready in heaven against the day when it will be brought on to the stage of history, not to snatch at visible status or power here and now. It might have been clearer if the passage had included verses 2–5 as well.

Proper 6

——— ∼ ———

1 Samuel 15.34—16.13
2 Corinthians 5.6–10[11–13]14–17
Mark 4.26–34

Once again the lectionary cuts Paul off just when he's getting interesting. Next week's passage starts at 6.1; what happened to 5.18–21, one of Paul's greatest summaries of his life and thought? However, the foothills that lead to this stunning mountain-top are themselves full of beauty and interest. Walking by faith, not by sight; appearing before the judgement-seat of Christ; the love of Christ constrains us; if anyone is in Christ, there is a new creation! As the old lady said of *Hamlet*, this passage is 'full of quotations'.

The theme is Paul's vindication of his own ministry, which the Corinthians had challenged, suggesting he was not as smooth or smart an operator as the teachers they now had. Paul doesn't care what they think; he and they must all be judged before the Messiah himself. He is who he is because he has been formed by the Messiah's love (v. 14), a love shown in death, evoking a response of self-giving love coupled with a re-evaluation of oneself and everybody else. Like someone feeling their way around a darkened room and finally, discovering the light, able to see everything clearly at last, so the estimates of other people that humans form in the darkness of prejudice are shown up when the light of the Messiah shines on them (v. 16). Paul had originally regarded even the Messiah in the old, prejudiced way. Now he was challenging the Corinthians to see everyone, himself included, not by the standards of their prevailing culture but in the light of the Messiah in whom all things had become new.

This up-ending of worldly ways of making judgements finds classic expression in David. Fresh-faced, energetic, ready for anything, he was so much the young shepherd that nobody had thought of summoning him home sooner. Mortals, the Lord reminded Samuel, look at outward appearances, but the Lord himself looks at the heart (16.7). David was good-looking as well, but that wasn't the point. God was searching for 'a man after his own heart' (1 Samuel 13.14). No early Christian could miss the overtones of what happened next. When he was anointed, YHWH's Spirit came upon him in power.

The contrast of outward appearances and God's strange hidden design is of course the subject of several parables, not least those in Mark 4. The seed grows secretly; the man who planted it doesn't know what's happening to it, which is ironic since he does every day what the seed is doing, going to bed and getting up (Mark 4.27). So too with the tiny mustard seed, which one might be tempted to scorn, like the Corinthians with Paul, not realizing what it would do next. Training the eye to look at things with faith and hope is not just a matter of Christian obedience. It is the way to overthrow prejudice and to see God's kingdom in unexpected places and people.

Proper 7

———— ∾ ————

1 Samuel 17.[1a, 4–11, 19–23] 32–49
2 Corinthians 6.1–13
Mark 4.35–41

Right from the start in Mark, Jesus is up against it. Tempted by Satan in the wilderness; shrieked at by benighted souls in the synagogue; criticized by the self-appointed religious experts. Now the sea itself, with all its dark and evil mythological overtones, rises up against him. And he is . . . asleep. There is as much mystery here as when the Word, through whom all things were created, lay asleep in his mother's arms.

The pattern, though, is familiar. David is anointed by Samuel and empowered by the Spirit, and here in the next chapter he is asking what Saul will give to the man who kills Goliath, and then enlisting to do exactly that. This launches him on a long career of opposition to the present regime, until at last the time comes for which, in the people's eyes, his victory over Goliath had prepared him, and he is anointed again as Israel's true and representative leader.

The evangelists, for whom Jesus' baptism was full of Davidic overtones, saw his subsequent career through that lens. What Mark conveys, in addition, is the sovereign freedom of Jesus in and through it all, sleeping through the storm and, when aroused, rebuking not only the wind and sea but also, because of their lack of faith, the disciples.

The poetical overtones of the storm on the lake (sea-monsters and so on, looking back at least to the crossing of the Red Sea) indicate what's going on, and point forwards to Mark's last scenes. The monsters conspire to send Jesus to sleep once and for all, only to find him waking on the third day and sending them packing. Like most Gospel stories, this one has a double effect: first, the sovereign and unrepeatable action of Jesus himself, like a boulder thrown into water from a great height, and, second, the waves and currents that splash outwards into the life of the Church.

The early Christians, reading Mark, would undoubtedly have thought of the Goliaths that lay in wait for them, challenging them and their God in the name of various kinds of paganism, forcing those anointed with the Spirit into a series of struggles that must often have felt as though they would be fatal. To them this story will have brought home once more the challenge to be faithful despite everything.

Thus, too, Paul's apostolic pilgrimage. Invoking Isaiah's servant-passages, he stands in the line of servant-messengers of God, battered yet still going forwards. The smooth stones he takes from the wadi are his sufferings and the fruits of the Spirit (look at the overlap between 2 Corinthians 6.6 and Galatians 5.22). With these to hand, he has no need of the heavy armour the Corinthians wanted him to wear, the sophisticated skills and tricks of the popular philosophers. The battle has now shifted to the hearts and lives of Christians themselves, and will be won by the weapons of the gospel and nothing else.

Proper 8

— ❧ —

2 Samuel 1.1, 17–27
2 Corinthians 8.7–15
Mark 5.21–43

Mark folds one story inside another, like someone tucking a second letter inside a first. (A Markan sandwich, some say; but food is important within the story itself, so let's not confuse the issue.) As in 2 Samuel, a double lament forms the backdrop for the new king to reveal his power.

The main, outer story is well known, but worth pondering. What did it cost Jairus, as a synagogue ruler, to seek Jesus' help? Why are Jesus' Aramaic words, *Talitha cum*, recorded, when almost all his other native speech is not? Why did Jesus tell them not to tell anyone? Is there any other story where the sovereignty and gentleness of Jesus are both on such equal, and integrated, display? When Jesus tells the parents to give their daughter some food, is Mark preparing us for 'You give them something to eat' in the next chapter? If so, so what? And, behind all these, more mysteriously: granted that many children must have died in Jesus' vicinity during his public career, why did he only do anything about it when, here and in Nain (Luke 7), it was brought to his attention?

Inside this story Mark has enfolded the intimate and surprising account of the woman with the 12-year haemorrhages (the years tally, of course, with the girl's age in the outer story). Nowhere else is Jesus' power described in such a physical way, so that when he is touched he can sense the release of healing energy. Nowhere else, perhaps, is it so clear that for him 'faith' could mean simply 'belief that I have the power to heal'. When Peter in Acts tells Cornelius the story of Jesus, this power forms a central part of the tale. It is a sign of God's anointing.

The story holds out comfort to those who cannot, as it were, march up and address Jesus. Enough to creep up behind and touch ... though don't be surprised if you're then gently but firmly brought out into the open. The whole passage invites slow meditation, identifying with one character after another, watching the unfolding scene through their eyes (including Jesus' – if you dare), and folding our stories in turn inside Mark's. Prepare for surprises.

A memory of Jesus' gentle sovereignty lingers in Paul's appeal to Corinth – which, incidentally, ought to be a comfort, and a lesson, to all ecclesiastical fund-raisers, not least unwilling ones. Paul takes two chapters in the middle of a deeply personal and theological letter to say that the church needs to have the cash ready when he comes, and preferably plenty of it; but he manages to say it without once mentioning 'money' as such. The motivation, he says, should be reflection on Jesus himself: he was rich, yet for your sakes became poor, so that you by his poverty might become rich. It's the same power-in-weakness theme which dominates 2 Corinthians, and it still takes us by surprise as it did Jairus and the rest.

Proper 9

— ∼ —

2 Samuel 5.1–5, 9–10
2 Corinthians 12.2–10
Mark 6.1–13

The paradoxes of power. David bided his time, refused to lift up his hand against God's anointed (though he knew himself to be anointed also), and then at last became king in a further anointing. The move to Jerusalem was politically shrewd (though obscured by the omission of verses 6–8): one of the last unconquered strongholds, it gave David a new capital independent of earlier tribal memories, as well as a victory which, completing Joshua's work, sealed David's royal vocation in the public eye.

And yet. When Jesus came to his home town he could do almost nothing. This strange inability, related to the faith, or lack of it, that he found, belongs with the whole theme of the Gospel. After all, when Jesus went to David's capital it was with different weapons, and to a different throne, from those of his ancestor. Yet it is in Jesus that God's spectacular promises to David, of perpetual world-wide dominion, have come true.

So different are their styles of kingship that many have doubted, what the New Testament is at pains to affirm, that Jesus' Davidic Messiahship remained of crucial significance. Power, like Messiahship itself, is redefined, but not abandoned, in the Gospel. It is not an exaggeration to say that the Church, oscillating (in Henry Chadwick's phrase) between the desire to rule the world and the desire to renounce it, has always struggled to work out what in practice this redefined Messiahship ought to mean.

It is a measure of Paul's theological insight that he was already grappling with this within thirty years of Jesus' death. He in turn has been woefully misunderstood here, and accused of subtle manipulation and cynical power-games.

The truth is very different. He is refusing to go along with the Corinthians' desire that he should be the kind of powerful apostle they had in mind. A more robustly Davidic leader would have suited them nicely. He will not play to the gallery that wants tales of spectacular spiritual triumphs. His greatest moment, he says, was a long time ago, and he's not allowed to say anything about it – except that he ended up limping, like Jacob after his encounter with God.

Paul had discovered that real power was hidden precisely in weakness. He learnt this with his head, we may suppose, when he encountered the crucified and risen Jesus on the road to Damascus; he learnt it with his body and his heart as he was thrown into jail, beaten up, abused and mocked. He discovered that when the Christ-pattern was thus stamped on him the power of the risen Christ came through as well, and he was able not only to work healings (he doesn't say much about that, but it seems to be presupposed) but also to exercise an effective servant-authority in the communities founded through his preaching.

If all this seems a long way removed from current questions about power structures in the Church, whose fault is that?

Proper 10

— ∿ —

2 Samuel 6.1–5, 12b–19
Ephesians 1.3–14
Mark 6.14–29

Two kings, a thousand years apart, and both in trouble at home. David brings God's ark into Jerusalem, and is so carried away with dancing and leaping before the Lord that his wife despises him, remembering no doubt the dignity of the former king, her father. Perhaps the narrator is already preparing us for the sad moment five chapters later, where David, successful and prosperous, sows the seeds of later disaster by seducing someone else's wife.

Plus ça change. Herod Antipas had taken his brother Philip's wife; a shrewd political move, most likely, as well as a passionate romance. Did Antipas still hope for recognition as the true Messiah? We can predict the reaction from the wild prophet by the river: how can this be the Lord's anointed?

Herod knows he's in trouble; John is a righteous and holy man, and many revere him as a prophet. He likes listening to him (an interesting comment from Mark, making Herod more than a one-dimensional villain) but is worried by what he hears. Then the birthday party: the wine, the guests, the girl, the disaster.

Now observe Great David's Greater Son (an ambiguous description if ever there was one), the Lord of the Dance, the one whom Herod considered a resurrected John the Baptist.

Nobody is yet saying he was the Messiah – they all think he's a prophet – yet Mark's readers know enough to see the way things are going. This is real kingship: Herod is a ghastly parody, even David only an oblique forerunner. And Mark's readers also realize that if the herald has come to a bad end at the hands of wicked people, the monarch may go the same way. If this is what happens to prophets, think what will happen to the king himself. This king, too, has been despised by his own family (3.31–5; 6.3–5), and will end up rejected by all. Paradoxical maybe, but this is the royal leadership for which Israel had waited a millennium.

But David really did bring the ark to Jerusalem, and throughout that millennium, with much joy and much sorrow, the people of Israel had gone there to worship the one true God, to tell the story of his mighty acts in the past and to pray for their completion in the future. Jerusalem was God's city, and David's city, and it was to Jerusalem that the new king would shortly be making his way to recapitulate those mighty acts, and to bring them to a new and unforeseen completion.

That completion gives Paul his vantage point. He tells the story, in the form of a great Jewish-style thanksgiving-prayer: 'Blessed be the God and Father of our Lord Jesus, the Messiah, who ...' has now accomplished the long-awaited purpose. It is the story of creation and exodus, of redemption and inheritance: the great Jewish story, now seen from a new angle, the redefined royal angle, the Messianic angle that never entered Herod's head.

Proper 11

—— ∾ ——

2 Samuel 7.1–14a
Ephesians 2.11–22
Mark 6.30–34, 53–56

Read 2 Samuel 7 through the eyes of a second-Temple Jew, and watch New Testament theology come into focus. This passage, read messianically at Qumran and elsewhere, fuses together four things. God promises David a perpetual royal line; a son who will build the Temple; a son who will be counted as God's son; and a son who will be 'raised up' (the Hebrew and Greek words in v. 12 could be read as 'I will resurrect'). This entire train of thought, reshaped around Jesus himself, was present in the mind of the early Church; see, for instance, Romans 1.3–4.

The passage turns on a pun. David, living in luxury while God's ark stays in a tent, proposes a house for God. 'House' can mean a building or a family, a 'royal house' either a palace or a lineage. God hears David's offer of a more permanent dwelling, but a true temple cannot start with human initiative. Nor, actually, can a building be the ultimate solution to the problem. God will raise up David's family; the son to be born will build the Temple; but the final response to David's underlying question is not bricks and mortar but a living human being, God's very self in human form. 'The glory of God', wrote Irenaeus, 'is the living man; and the life of man is the vision of God.'

The Temple, then, became the home of God's glory. But

the early Christians believed that, as always intended, this glory had now taken up permanent residence in Jesus. This early, high, deeply Jewish Christology was rooted, via passages like this, in the belief that the Temple-promises of the Old Testament had come true not in a building but in a human being.

With similar speed, they concluded that those who were 'in the Messiah' were likewise the temple of God's glory, through the Spirit of Jesus which lived in them. This, particularly in 1 Corinthians and, as here, in Ephesians, became a source of early ecumenical theology: the single temple, built of different bricks, has no dividing wall, as did the Jerusalem Temple, to separate Jews from Gentiles (or, for that matter, one to separate women from men, but that isn't the point here). Precisely because the Messiah took the hostility of the two groups upon himself, caught as he was in the crossfire of Roman intransigence, Jewish popular revolution, and Jewish aristocratic power-games, he has abolished the symbolic universe, represented by the Torah as well as the Temple, in which Jew and Gentile were locked into irrevocable hostility, and has achieved what the God of Israel always intended: a new humanity. Notice how even within the temple-metaphor the underlying thought remains human; the structure 'grows into a holy Temple in the Lord' (v. 21).

Like an art thief taking the canvas but leaving the woodwork, today's Gospel omits the story, replacing it next week with someone else's version, and leaves the framework. No comment.

Proper 12

—— ∾ ——

2 Samuel 11.1–15
Ephesians 3.14–21
John 6.1–21

Think of the Lord's Prayer while reading Ephesians 3. Paul prays to the Father, from whom all fatherhood 'in heaven and on earth' is named, that he will give us ... all things in Christ, because to him belong the power and the glory for ever, Amen. Perhaps this, along with John 17, is one of the earliest expanded meditations on the great prayer.

If so, the bit we're missing in the middle nicely corresponds to the story in John 6 (replacing Mark's version in our sequence of readings). Give us this day ... but what they wanted was not food, but a king and a kingdom. The sign, not only the bread and the fish but also the twelve baskets left over, did not appear out of the blue to people watching to see what a conjuror would do next for their entertainment. It was given to people hungry for Israel's restoration, eager for a king to give them Passover-food, freedom, power and glory. That was the context within which they saw the sign, and it was almost too much.

In the evening, Jesus and his followers enacted the remaining part of the prayer. Evil, in the form of wind and wave, threatened to engulf them, but Jesus came to them on the water. (When will someone have the courage to translate *ego eimi* in this passage as 'It's me!'?) If the kingdom really is invading hostile territory with God's power, we should expect to be tested, to need to pray for deliverance. Paul prays not for bread, forgiveness and safety but for strength, for the indwelling of the Messiah, and for God's powerful love to sweep us off our feet.

All this makes the story of David and Bathsheba, and the sorry stories of our own day inside the Church as well as outside, the more shocking. Is Paul's vision of the moral power of God, living within Christians through the Spirit, simply unrealistic?

Many would say No. As every spiritual director knows, for every Christian who has followed David down the easy road to short-term pleasure and long-term disaster there are many with the same opportunities and temptations but who have found the way of escape, often to their own surprise. Moral courage and God's power are strange and sometimes apparently unpredictable, but they are realities none the less.

Within the wider narrative of 2 Samuel, David's double sin (adultery plus murder) is the point from which his other failures begin to emerge, resulting in Absalom's rebellion, public humiliation (not that the palace would be ignorant of what had happened that spring afternoon), civil war, the decimation of his family, and squabbles over succession. As often in scripture, the wider fate of the people of God is nicely balanced with their private lives. The Church has often found it difficult to address both simultaneously, but both Testaments, not least in the Lord's Prayer itself, hold them together as two necessary parts of the same reality.

Proper 13

— ∾ —

2 Samuel 11.26—12.13a
Ephesians 4.1–16
John 6.24–35

Hands up those who took one look at this week's Old
Testament lesson and gave it a wide berth. All right; now
hands up those who seized upon it as a chance to preach on
How Not To Commit Immorality. Full marks to the lectionary for including one of the Bible's shockers – though not
for losing its nerve and stopping, like Britten's *Rape of
Lucretia*, just before the deed itself.

The point, of course, is neither to draw a veil over such
incidents, nor to wallow in wickedness, but to reflect with
sober sorrow on the larger story that here turns a fateful
corner. David's own immorality and violence have set a tone;
he can't now stop his sons going the same route. Absalom,
Tamar's full brother, takes murderous vengeance on Amnon,
starting the rebellion which tears the heart out of David's
kingship. David's sins find him out, by a long and shamefully
public process of feuding in the family – from which,
according to the promises made so soon before, God
would raise up the coming great king. Private lives and
public events cannot be separated. You cannot partition
integrity any more than you can fence off part of the sea.

It is that wholeness of genuinely human life, in both
personal and corporate aspects, that Paul describes in the
majestic exhortation of Ephesians 4. Each is given a gift, but

the gifts together make up the single body of Christ. Selfish impurity breeds corporate disintegration (4.17–24, omitted from the sequence of readings, might be a comment on Amnon and his successors ever since); personal holiness (which includes gentleness and humility) leads to mutual upbuilding and unity.

It doesn't take much reflection to see where our own society is in all of this, not least in the way that sin and selfishness deceive, darken understanding, and twist logic so that people start to believe good is evil and evil good. Inside the Church as well as outside, there are such things as trickery, cunning, and pseudo-doctrines which carry off those who lack the maturity to spot the flaw. Teaching and leadership are what's needed, and what's given in Christ; they are the marks, and the means, of the community which reflects the renewing and transforming love of God.

All this, of course, needs faith. Jesus challenges the puzzled crowd to see through the physical loaves to the true bread beyond. How easy for us to over-spiritualize, to suppose that Jesus is unconcerned with earthly bread (feeding a crowd would be an odd way to make that point). The God-given earthly world functions as an icon or sacrament of the heavenly, which intermingles with the earthly and gives it its full meaning. Greedy abuse of the physical world makes dualists out of the morally sensitive. Jesus invites his hearers to trust him, the Word made flesh, to taste in him the bread of life, and to find heaven and earth united in the promised kingdom.

Proper 14

—— ∿ ——

2 Samuel 18.5–9, 15, 31–33
Ephesians 4.25—5.2
John 6.35, 41–51

Come, believe, and eat. Simple yet profound, carrying us with characteristic Johannine effortlessness from bread by the lake to the bread of life. The bridge between them is Jesus himself, who will give his flesh, that which the Word had become (1.14), for the life of the world.

The physical and spiritual, the bread Moses gave and the true bread that Jesus gives, must be held together around the person of Jesus himself. We cannot collapse it into the idea that the physical is irrelevant and the spiritual all-important. To 'come' to Jesus means to approach Jesus himself, not some Jesus-fantasy that could be pulled into new shapes at will. The hope is not disembodied eternity but bodily resurrection (6.44). To 'believe' in Jesus means to grasp, with heart, intellect and will, that in this human being the true and living God is fully and personally present.

'Justification by faith', though the phrase is Paul's, summarizes John's message too. Those who believe – and 'believe' isn't a general religious attitude to life, but the specific faith that embraces Jesus himself as the bread of life – are marked as God's people in the present, and assured of the (newly embodied) life of the age to come. This Johannine emphasis is controversial (verses 41–3) for the same reason as Paul's: if this faith is the key to it all, it is open to everyone, irrespective of ethnic origin. The cost of this breathtaking inclusivity is, as always, the humiliating exclusivity of the focus on Jesus and his death. Otherwise 'Jesus' becomes a cipher for whatever makes us feel good at the time.

Take all this theology, turn it into a story and a symbol, and you have John 6 in a nutshell, or perhaps a breadbasket. The eucharist cannot have been far from John's mind, and that of his readers, and its meaning is given by Jesus himself, and the faith which comes to him. Jesus' forthcoming death (6.51) is the clue to it all. They had wanted to make him king (6.15), but Jesus' royal claim would be that he had done what his ancestor had wanted to do: 'Would I had died instead of you, O Absalom, my son, my son'.

To live within this story, to make it one's own in prayer and eucharist, in devotion to Jesus himself, is to find the key to that way of life, startling and subversive in the world of Graeco-Roman paganism, that Paul describes in Ephesians 5. Just as radical as giving up immorality (the previous and following paragraphs) is the challenge to abandon lying and bitterness. This isn't simply a call to 'be nice to people' as a matter of ethical effort (though, to paraphrase Charlie Brown, being nice to people ain't everything, but being nasty to people ain't anything). It's a call to copy God – the God whose startling love has been fully unveiled in the cross of the true King.

Proper 15

— ∾ —

1 *Kings* 2.10–12; 3.3–14
Ephesians 5.15–20
John 6.51–58

A glance at the bits of 1 Kings 1—3 which are not read in this sequence will explain why Solomon so desperately needed wisdom. His father's victories, though remarkable, could not be relied on for long-term security. His own family, whose struggles over the succession had soured his rise to power, could certainly be relied on for long-term squabbles. The coalition of Israelite tribes, held together around the non-tribal capital of Jerusalem, was under strain even in David's day. If ever a young leader needed wisdom, it was Solomon.

The fact that he met these challenges, postponing the break-up of the fragile kingdom through a long reign, is itself a sign that his perennial reputation for wisdom is justified. And of course the main achievement of that wisdom was the building of the Temple. Here we find several elements of later Jewish thinking: wisdom as God's handmaid, given to enable humans to be co-creators of God's intended projects; the Temple itself as the place of God's dwelling, of worship, prayer and sacrifice; David's son and heir bringing the two together, as long as he fulfils the law. Half of New Testament Christology is stored away in this narrative, laid up like a fine wine for a thousand years.

Solomon's humility and wisdom contrast sharply with the arrogance and bumbling short-termism we find in much ancient and modern history. What might it take to get us back on track?

Paul's recipe for wisdom is bracing. Avoid the folly of comfortable, and fashionable, immorality (Ephesians 5.3–14, which forms the backdrop to this exhortation to wisdom). Make the most of the time (literally, 'buy it back'; assume it's being snatched from you, and get it back under your control). Understand God's will: think it through and see where it conflicts with the easy option. Glad and grateful worship takes priority over booze and sleaze. Think of the pagan rulers, and their imitators, of Paul's day, and perhaps our own as well, and you'll see what a contrast he is recommending.

But it can only be attempted by those who, through that thankful worship, are being fed on the bread and wine which is Jesus himself. Wisdom, Temple and Torah point forward to the one who offers his own flesh and blood as food and drink.

This shocking affront to Jewish sensibilities (cannibalism? drinking blood? No wonder they found it hard to take) is meant to jolt us into recognizing what is in fact being said. Solomon's prayer for God's wisdom was a prayer for God's own life, God's own second self, to live within him, clothing itself with his thinking, his decisions, his leadership. Our feeding on Jesus, in the eucharist of course but in so many other ways too, is our prayer for God's own life, made flesh in Jesus, to clothe itself afresh with us, to get (as we say) into our bones and our bloodstreams, our thinking, our decisions, our leadership.

Proper 16

———— ∾ ————

1 Kings 8.[1, 6, 10–11]22–30, 41–43
Ephesians 6.10–20
John 6.56–69

Jesus returns, at the end of the long 'bread of life' discourse, to the central thrust. Don't look for more loaves and fishes; look for the different dimension of life which the Son of Man offers, the dimension which will be signalled by his eventual exaltation to be with the Father.

All very well, but today's hearers are almost bound to misunderstand. 'The spirit gives life; the flesh is useless'; fine, we think, and off we go with Plato into radical dualism. Don't worry, we think, about the world of space, time and matter; concern yourself with the world of pure spirit.

The problem is that 'spirit', here and elsewhere, is not the opposite of 'matter', morally or ontologically. The Jewish way of life – Temple, food laws and all – was commanded and blessed by the same creator God who made the physical world and called it good, the same God whose Word has now become flesh, flesh that will rise from the dead and go to the Father. This is the God whose Spirit fills the word 'spiritual' with its true meaning. In Jesus, as in the Temple, flesh and spirit, heaven and earth, have been brought together once and for all.

Of course, if you try to live on the material level alone it will become 'flesh' in the negative sense, corruptible and corrupting. But in John, as in Paul (despite repeated assertions to the contrary), and as indeed throughout Genesis to Revelation, the two spheres of God's created and glorious world, the earthly and the heavenly, are made to interlock, to work in intricate harmony.

That's why Paul's warning about the battle Christians face is not about escaping from the (evil) physical sphere into the (good) spiritual sphere. The spiritual sphere is precisely where you meet the worst foes, the foes of which even Caesar and his brutal henchmen are just pale copies. 'Spiritual warfare' conjures up bizarre images today: Superman-like characters flying around the sky blitzing pterodactyl-like demons with supernatural ray-guns. But just because *Jaws* was over the top, that doesn't mean sharks don't eat people. Just because some people cherish ludicrous and caricatured fantasies about spiritual warfare, that doesn't mean Paul is talking nonsense. Anyone who genuinely tries to take two steps forward for the kingdom of God will know that there are unseen forces which try to drag you back at least one step, possibly three.

The weapons for the battle are not showy, flashy, or Hollywood-friendly. They are sober, almost boring, mostly defensive. The belt of truth. The breastplate of justice. The shoes of the gospel of peace. The shield of faith. The helmet of salvation. And – the only attacking weapon – the Spirit's sword, God's word. All to be surrounded with prayer.

Think back to Ephesians' earlier statement about the Church as God's renewed Temple. Now read 1 Kings 8 again, and ask yourself what it would mean to be builders, dedicators, guardians and worshippers in this Temple today.

99

Proper 17

—— ∼ ——

Song of Solomon 2.8–13
James 1.17–27
Mark 7.1–8, 14–15, 21–23

The main bit missing from Mark 7 is about nullifying God's word through human tradition. Hmmm.

Granted, there are two different issues at stake here: cleanness and uncleanness (with a further subdivision: clean hands and clean food), and tradition versus Scripture. But even supposing we highlight the first, omitting verses 9–13, we cannot understand Mark's point without the transition in verse 17, and his own comment in verse 19. Let's put this right before we too end up making a tradition of misreading Scripture.

The point of the passage, for Mark, is that Jesus couldn't say in public what he says here in private. Think of the Maccabaean martyrs, dying rather than defile themselves with unclean food. Think of Daniel 1, where the heroes don't die, but will shortly face pagan persecution. Remember how such stories function in a beleaguered community (think of Belfast or Bosnia, where tales of atrocity and heroism, like a blaze in a forest, can leap across the fire-break of centuries and spark fresh fury and enthusiasm). Think of first-century Jews in 'Galilee of the Gentiles', fiercely maintaining their loyalty to God and the Torah. And now imagine Jesus saying casually to all and sundry (as the lectionary makes him do) that unclean food cannot defile a person. He's asking to be lynched.

Mark is emphatic: this sort of thing could only be said in private. And even then Jesus is cryptic with his explanation, so that Mark himself has to rub home the point. This means that all foods are clean.

Only now can we face the real problem: the food-laws are not 'tradition', they're Scripture. Does that mean that Jesus is doing the very thing he is rebuking them for?

The answer cannot be simply that Jesus has the right to set aside even Scripture. That isn't incarnate sovereignty, it's cavalier casualness. What we find, instead, is Jesus' strong sense of *what time it is*. It's time for the kingdom of God to break in. And when that happens, laws which had a strong point as part of God's preparation are no longer needed.

God was now calling all people, not just Jews, to belong to his people; because God was now dealing with the root disease of humanity, the problem resident in every human heart. The time had come to blow out the candles and watch the sun rise. Scripture would be truly fulfilled when that to which the purity laws pointed – God's longing that his people be holy through and through – was achieved. James speaks of the perfect law being that which makes people doers as well as hearers. However accurate the signposts are, you don't need them once you've arrived at your destination.

Remember this subversive Jesus when you think of the traditional interpretation of the Song of Songs, in which he is the Bridegroom. His message? The time has come. Everything is now going to be different. If this is romance, it's based on realism.

Proper 18

— ～ —

Proverbs 22.1–2, 8–9, 22–23
James 2.1–10[11–13], 14–17
Mark 7.24–37

James' comments about faith and works, part of his wide-ranging application of 'the law of liberty' (1.25, 2.12), have become famous because of their apparent contradiction of Paul's insistence on justification by faith alone. Perhaps that's why his strong emphasis on the 'no favourites in church' rule (2.1–7) has so often been ignored; if Luther said James was an epistle of straw, who are we to take him seriously? Thus the entire Wisdom tradition in both Testaments (consider James' closeness to Proverbs, in both style and content) is often set aside.

Here, though, it is Luther, not James, who is made of straw. When James says 'faith' he means a verbal formula, intellectual consent to Jewish monotheism (2.15, 19); for Paul 'faith' is the response of 'faith*fulness*' which God sought from Israel, found in Jesus, and evokes through the gospel. When James speaks of 'works' he means neither the attempt to earn one's own salvation by moral effort, nor the attempt to confine God's grace to those who can perform 'works of Torah', i.e. Jews. Rather, he means the outward effects that faith must have if it is to be genuine – what Paul himself calls 'faith working through love' (Galatians 5.6). James and Paul, in different ways, are opposing Jewish attempts to seek security in ethnic identity without the need for the life-changing grace unveiled in Jesus.

What's more, James' main concern is salvation (2.14), that is, *final* justification, which Paul also aligns with good works (Romans 2.6–11, also interestingly in a context where 'no partiality' is a major theme). When Paul speaks of 'justification by faith' in Romans and Galatians, he is speaking of the *present* justification which anticipates that final verdict. Paul and James are singing different parts within the wider harmony of the gospel.

That harmony includes Mark 7 as well. Jesus has placed a time-bomb beside those Jewish institutions that stressed ethnic separateness; he is now confronted with the need to explode it, sooner than expected. 'You can't give the children's bread to the dogs'; a harsh saying, hardly one the early Christians would have invented, but turning quickly into warm acceptance of Gentile faith. Though Jesus (like many Jews of the day) clearly envisaged a future time when Gentiles would come to share the blessings of the kingdom (think of the centurion's servant, and Jesus' comments on that incident in Matthew 8.10–12), he seems to be surprised that it is all happening this quickly. No more privilege for the 'children'; all can be healed, all must hear, and soon.

The kingdom is rushing forwards, and it is imperative that he teach the disciples its meaning as soon as possible. Mark, here as elsewhere, uses the story of the deaf-mute as part of his build-up to the time when the disciples, in the next chapter, will hear plainly, and be able to speak the truth about Jesus.

Proper 19

—— ✳ ——

Proverbs 1.20–33
James 3.1–12
Mark 8.27–38

The first nine chapters of Proverbs introduce two personified figures: Lady Wisdom and Mistress Folly. Both appeal to 'the sons of men'; we had better not try, in the interests of inclusivity, to flatten out the genders, since they are part of the point. The discourse winds to and fro between the Lady and the Mistress, both as metaphors for the appeal of Wisdom and Folly in every area of life, and as a metonymy in which sexual morality is a key illustrative aspect of human decision-making.

The underlying counsel (1.7) is that the fear of YHWH is the beginning of wisdom ('fear' here, of course, means awe and reverence before God's greatness, sovereignty and holiness, not cowering away from an unpredictable bully). The premise, and promise, is that YHWH is the creator God in whose image humans are made. To worship him is to become more truly human, more fully what one was meant and made to be.

If humans are made to reflect God's image into his world, then wisdom, the one through whom that world was created (8.22–31), is precisely what they need. Wisdom will be given to those who fear YHWH so that they can understand how his world works and act appropriately, and indeed joyfully, within it. This is the fountainhead from which flow the later, often apparently random, streams of advice, collected from many sources but now made available through the fear of YHWH.

James, the New Testament's nearest approach to Proverbs in style and content, picks up in this chapter the regular theme of human speech, with its huge potential for good and ill. Jesus had warned of judgement on the basis of one's words (Matthew 12.36–7); James warns of the danger of inconsistent speech to one's neighbour, and even to God. The untameable tongue can set things ablaze. Those who use words for a living are in special danger.

The underlying theology concerns speech as a key part of the image-bearing capacity of humans, reflecting the God who is not silent but reveals himself in words, and ultimately in the Word. We are so aware of the dangers and limitations of our own words that we sometimes try to rescue God from the same problem. The fault, however, is not with God's habit of speech, but with our inability to reflect him truly and appropriately.

Peter's words, blurted out finally after a long and slow process of education (see Mark 8.14–26, a careful setting of the scene for this climax), illustrate the point nicely. He is right to declare that Jesus is Messiah, but wrong to project on to him his own distorted (though conventional) ideas about what Messiahship might mean. Jesus' vocation will stand conventional wisdom on its head. The way of the cross is the true, though shocking, reflection of God's thoughts. Peter must learn to renounce conventional, skin-saving folly and to walk the steep path of subversive wisdom.

Proper 20

—— ∽ ——

Proverbs 31.10–31
James 3.13—4.3, 7–8a
Mark 9.30–37

Fortunately, Jesus stopped the disciples in their tracks
before they acted out James 4 as well as James 3. Envy
and selfish ambition, yes; but covetousness had not yet
led to murder. The internecine strife in Jerusalem 40 years
later (just after James was writing?) shows how easily it
could have happened. Do, please, read the missing verses
from James (4.4–6, 8b–10), and allow them to colour
your hearing of the gospel. Who is God's friend, and
who God's enemy, and where is this drama worked out
today?

Classic Markan irony: Jesus telling the disciples about his
approaching death, the disciples arguing over who was the
greatest. Mark insists that they couldn't understand him;
what might they have thought he meant? Jesus so often spoke
figuratively that it's not surprising his literal sense (betrayed,
killed, rising again) was too much for them to swallow. Was
he perhaps talking about the suffering that would herald the
arrival of the kingdom? Well, yes, but not the way they
thought.

Jesus' response, using the child as both example and
promise, comes across as oblique. We expect teaching
about humility, as in the similar incident in 10.13–16. But
this is different. Why does Jesus speak of 'receiving' a child in

his name? How does that address their wrong attitude, or encourage them to the right one?

They were each hoping, it seems, to become Jesus' official spokesman. Jesus would be king; the question was, who would be Chief of Staff, head of the royal household? Who would speak for Jesus? Who would be his ambassador, welcomed with the honour due to Jesus himself? Answer: anyone at all, and the humbler the better. An insignificant, unnamed child can become Jesus' official representative, so that receiving him or her means receiving Jesus. Furthermore (a claim heavy with Johannine-style christological implications) by receiving Jesus, not least in the person of an insignificant child, people will receive 'the one who sent him'. Friendship with God is on offer, as in James, but it will mean turning one's back on friendship with the world and its expectations.

James is the New Testament's chief 'wisdom' book, and in Proverbs 31 we have one of the genre's crowning moments. The earlier chapters contrast Lady Wisdom and Mistress Folly, and here at last personified wisdom becomes a real person: a cheerful, independent-minded, multi-skilled wife, whose life is by no means restricted to managing her own household, though of course she does that, but who runs a business (v. 18) and cares for the poor (v. 20). Of course, as the cynics point out, this is a man's view of what a good woman does; but let's give credit where credit is due. If more Christian teaching about the role of women had started from Proverbs, fewer mistakes would have been made. And if the disciples had had an ounce of the wisdom Proverbs offers, their conversation with Jesus might have gone somewhat differently.

Proper 21

———— ∿ ————

Esther 7.1–6, 9–10
James 5.13–20
Mark 9.38–50

The ancient world was full of stories in which the threatened hero or heroine is rescued at last, and the people who had almost overcome them are condemned instead. David kills Goliath. Homer's heroes – some of them, anyway – defeat their rivals after tense battles. The Son of Man is exalted, the Beast destroyed. Plenty of plays and novels follow the same line. We tell the story of the twentieth century in similar terms: think of Hitler, or Mussolini.

So why do we find Esther chapter 7 hard to take? The vengeance is stark and shocking, particularly when two verses are removed (typical: they refer to Haman's supposed attack on Esther's virtue). Haman is hanged on the gallows he had prepared for Mordecai, Esther's uncle. Rough justice at best, we think; at worst a bad-tempered lynching. This impression isn't helped if you go, as I once did in Jerusalem at the height of the intifada, to a Purim celebration, where the whole book is read, and discover that at this point in the story crowds of children with toy trumpets and drums raise the roof in celebration. My host on that occasion, a learned Jewish scholar, leant over to me and muttered 'I never like this bit'. Neither did I.

Haman had of course asked for it. He had plotted a major pogrom against a large and widespread Jewish community.

Not for nothing have twentieth-century Jews felt history repeating itself, with Hitler partially succeeding where Haman failed. But what does the Gospel say?

Well, not exactly what we might think. The worm is turning in our sensibilities, and some of the finest theologians are now reminding us that being nice to everybody, seeking reconciliation at any price, has to be balanced by naming, and dealing with, evil. Even in the last chapter of James, where forgiveness, healing and the restoration of sinners are the order of the day, the great example of fervent prayer is Elijah; and a glance at his story will reveal that the decisive moment in the coming of the rain was the slaughter of the prophets of Baal. And in Mark 9, with its tender care for 'the little ones who believe in me', there are ominous words about millstones around necks and unquenchable fire.

The problem seems to be that, when people give themselves to the practice of genuine wickedness, a good God must hate, and deal with, not only the sin but the sinner; but that those who follow the crucified Christ (upon whom the Haman-like, contemptuous wrath of Rome had fallen) are forbidden to seek or practise revenge on their own account. Omit the first, and the cry for justice will rise higher than our squeamish sentiment. Omit the second, and you sprinkle holy water on the lynch mobs. Leaving vengeance to God, as Paul instructs (Romans 12.19–21), was revolutionary then and remains so today. It doesn't mean denying that evil is real and that God hates it.

Proper 22

—— ∼ ——

Job 1.1; 2.1–10
Hebrews 1.1–4; 2.5–12
Mark 10.2–16

Angels are one thing; angels as God's heavenly council, discussing policy, are another; 'the Accuser' (the word 'Satan' is a title before it is a proper name) as himself an angel, a celestial Director of Public Prosecutions, is harder still; God giving this DPP carte blanche to see if he can find a charge against an unsuspecting human – well, this is beyond the pale. Yet this is what we see, as the prologue to Job takes us round to the back of the stage. Behind the drama and debate of Job and his friends, this is what is 'really' going on.

One might, of course, say that if you don't like what Job says about the problem of evil you're at liberty to offer an alternative. Answers on a postcard, please. But part of the answer is that there isn't an 'answer' in any sense that would 'solve' the problem; the book is, rather, a fuller way of stating the problem itself. Until we have all the dimensions before us we don't know what we're talking about – if indeed talking is the most appropriate thing to do.

Jesus, after all, didn't talk about 'the problem of evil' in that sense. He lived, breathed, taught and eventually died for the Kingdom of God, God's saving sovereignty over evil on earth and in heaven. Juxtaposing Job and Hebrews, as we now begin to do, produces some interesting reflected light: Jesus wasn't an angel, not least because, for the task he had to accomplish, it was necessary as well as appropriate for him to be fully human. (Appropriate, because the one who was from all eternity the true reflection of God (1.3) became the truly human one, that is, the one who reflects God's image.)

It isn't, then, that Jesus offers an abstract or intellectual answer to Job's problem. Jesus, we might say, had to *become* Job, suffering unjustly at the hands of the powers, 'in order that by God's grace he might taste death for everyone' (2.9). A 'solution', it seems, doesn't mean 'a theoretical framework within which it all makes rational sense'. In God's many-sided world, solutions take the form of a living embodiment of God's healing love and power.

That living embodiment challenges today's world, as it did Jesus', with his words about divorce (and about children). The Pharisees' question was political, not just about abstract ethics: remember why John was imprisoned and beheaded, look where Mark locates this story (10.1), and reflect on the trap set for John's cousin. Again, 'the solution' isn't a theoretical framework, but a life reflecting God's image. God's will in creation, for man and woman to become one flesh, is not set aside by a Mosaic permission 'given because of your hardheartedness'. The implication, shocking and difficult then and now, is that Jesus, restoring God's creation to its original intention, is offering a cure for hardness of heart. Once the word becomes flesh, solutions must be more than words.

Proper 23

—— ❧ ——

Job 23.1–9, 16–17
Hebrews 4.12–16
Mark 10.17–31

Two moments jump out at us from this intense little drama.
Jesus looks at the man and loves him; not, perhaps, our
natural reaction to someone claiming to keep six out of ten
commandments perfectly. (A pity Job 23.11–12 is omitted,
since there Job says much the same thing.) The disciples are
flabbergasted at Jesus' comment about camels and needles;
not, surely, our natural reaction to being warned about the
danger of riches (we've heard all that before, but they clearly
hadn't).

These flashes warn us that the story isn't saying what we
expect. We assume the man will be asking 'how to go to
heaven when he dies'. He isn't, and Jesus doesn't tell him
that. The journey he wants is horizontal, not vertical. God
will bring in his kingdom, the Age to Come; heaven will
arrive on earth; some will be adjudged worthy to inherit this
new world. This isn't 'eternal life' as in 'timeless existence',
but 'the full life of the Coming Age' ('eternal' is from the
same root as 'age'). 'Treasure in heaven' isn't something you
go to heaven to enjoy, any more than having money in the
bank means you have to spend it in the bank. It's waiting for
you against the day when heaven and earth become one.

Jesus' response, too, is hardly what you'd expect. 'Keep
the commandments?' Hadn't Jesus read Luther? Why not

'believe the gospel'? Answer: because part of the question is, what does it mean to be a true Jew, who will be vindicated when God finally acts? The definition of Jewishness focused on keeping Torah; Jesus has come, not to abolish it, but to fulfil it. The gospel is new, but it's not merely novel.

But notice which commandments Jesus *doesn't* quote (there is an extra problem, as to whether 'don't defraud' is meant to cover the last commandment; we can leave that to one side). What's happened to the first four? The sabbath is not mentioned; no surprises there for Mark's readers. But what about the first three: No gods before YHWH? No graven images? No taking YHWH's name in vain?

The answer is world-shaking. Jesus substitutes three things for the opening words of the Sinaitic covenant: sell up, give it away, follow me. The commandments have become devastatingly simple and personal. The implication, as with the divorce discussion earlier in the chapter, is that Jesus is moving beyond the Mosaic covenant into a new area, as indeed you'd expect if the Age to Come is being born. And behind that again there looms up the suggestion, like a great cathedral suddenly emerging out of a thick mist ahead of you: loyalty to Jesus now functions as the loyalty which Israel's God demands to him and him alone.

This is one of those stories that, as Hebrews says, divides between joints and marrow. Happily, the same Jesus who demands this complete allegiance is there also as the one who sympathizes with our weaknesses.

Proper 24

———— ∿ ————

Job 38.1–7 [34–41]
Hebrews 5.1–10
Mark 10.35–45

'Were you there,' asks the old song, 'when they crucified my Lord?' 'Were you there,' the Lord enquires of Job, 'when I laid the foundation of the earth?' Both questions receive the answer 'No', but for different reasons; born too late in one case, born as a human creature in the other. Yet both questions are invitations, not simply put-downs. You need to ponder what you missed.

Of course, in Job's case it is a put-down as well. The majestic stride through the glories of creation – stars, sea, snow, animals, birds, and finally Leviathan itself (chapter 41) – compels Job into appropriate humility. It isn't so much an answer to his nagging question as a statement of why the question cannot be answered, or not yet. It's a way of saying that God's ways are not our ways, and that the right path lies in submission to the strange wisdom by which the world was made.

From this point of view it isn't so much a matter, as some have said, of Jesus providing the answer to the questions Job was asking, though in some ways that's true too. It is rather, we might say, that Jesus *became* Job, 'learning obedience through the things he suffered', as Hebrews starkly puts it. God was able to save him from death. But Jesus, shouting and weeping in prayer (an important and often ignored historical memory, presumably of Gethsemane), fought his way to costly submission to the divine purpose which was taking him *through* death and into the world of new creation. God was laying the foundations of the new earth, giving the morning stars a new song to sing, taming Leviathan at last.

James and John, like Job, come with the wrong question. They weren't there when God determined on the plan of salvation, and they won't be there when their Lord is crucified. They'll be hiding like rats in a hole, unable (for the moment at least) to drink the cup or share the baptism. Their squabble with the other disciples, like Job's with his comforters, simply keeps the misunderstandings in circulation. They need to be silent before the unimagined, unlooked-for fresh revelation of upside-down divine wisdom. The world goes about things in one way; God does it differently.

When Jesus explains the necessity of the cross he starts with a *political* point. Leviathan, whether the sea-monster or the political 'absolute state', must be tamed, but can only be tamed by the God revealed in the suffering Son of Man. Hobbes, not for the last time, needs to be corrected by Calvin. Isaiah's vision of the Servant will indeed be fulfilled in Jesus; but this was never simply about sinful souls being saved by an arbitrary substitute. It was always about YHWH, the sovereign one, defeating the gods that have enslaved his people and, redeeming them, renewing not only the covenant but creation itself. Were you there? No, but follow this path and you will be.

The Last Sunday After Trinity

—— ∾ ——

Job 42.1–6, 10–17
Hebrews 7.23–28
Mark 10.46b–52

Three very different prayers.

Whatever we think of the ending of the book of Job (some scholars, inevitably, suppose it a later addition; some in our gloomy culture think it spoils the story to have Job so splendidly restored), the turning-point in his story should not be missed. He repents of his own presuming to question God – though God himself declares that he has in fact spoken the truth, that is, that he has maintained God's justice against superficial caricatures – and he prays for his friends, guilty of those same untrue caricatures. The prayer, for the people who had been torturing him with their spurious 'comfort', is itself an act born of the humility that accepts God's justice even when it doesn't understand it. Swift restoration now follows.

Somehow, God's justice is at work not as a blind force out beyond Job and his friends, but as a strange presence, inviting them in their own relationships to taste the humility, but also the new power, it brings to those who cast themselves upon it. Prayer, indeed, depends upon God's reliability and justice; if God were capricious or unjust, it would be better to remain silent. Job's prayer embodies not only his own forgiveness of his friends, but also his new, humble trust in God's reliability.

Intercession for his people is the central task of the Christ of Hebrews. The long passage about Jesus' fulfilment of the Melchizedek promise in Psalm 110 focuses finally on this point: the priest is there to plead to God on behalf of his people, and Jesus fulfils this role perfectly because, as the psalm says, he holds his royal priesthood in perpetuity. Unlike the levitical priests – and unlike Job – he has no sins of his own to deal with first. His central task, acted out physically on Calvary and embodied thereafter in his representative role in the heavenly realms, is to come before the Father with his sinful people on his heart. Nor is this, as in some iconography, a matter of his plaintively presenting his own suffering before an otherwise stern and unyielding Father. The Father himself appointed him for this purpose, so that we should have complete assurance of salvation, being in no doubt of his eternal and all-powerful saving love for us.

That same saving love, embodied in the Jesus who has set his face towards the cross, stands by the gate of Jericho as blind Bartimaeus shouts for mercy and refuses to be silenced. This time the intercession is for himself, simple, direct, and full of faith: 'Teacher, I want to see again.' (Jesus had asked him what he wanted; 'Have mercy on me', from a roadside beggar, would normally mean cash, but this request was altogether different.) From the complexities of Job, through the ministry of Jesus Christ himself, to the simplicity of Bartimaeus: coming before God in prayer is the central God-given human task, the one by which, whether spectacularly or quietly, everything is transformed.

Sundays Before Advent

The Fourth Sunday
Before Advent

—— ∾ ——

Deuteronomy 6.1–9
Hebrews 9.11–14
Mark 12.28–34

For once the lectionary hits the jackpot. These readings
dovetail perfectly, revealing powerfully the continuity and
discontinuity between Christianity and the Old Testament.

The key is the bit we might miss if we weren't alerted to it.
Only Mark records the little exchange between Jesus and the
scribe, which shows how the question about the great commandment fits into the whole sequence of thought. Mark
11—13 is framed by Jesus' action in the Temple (a symbolic
warning of its destruction), and by the prophetic discourse
on the Mount of Olives. The intervening material, including
this passage, is not simply a string of miscellaneous con-
troversies. It all explains the same point: what Jesus is doing
will take the place of the Temple. From here there is a
straight line to Jesus' hearing before the High Priest, at which
the question of the Temple is central, and thence to his death,
through which (Mark implies) all is accomplished.

Jesus' initial answer is apparently conventional. The
Shema prayer, starting with Deuteronomy 6, was already
central to Jewish devotion. Wholehearted love of God, and of
one's neighbour as oneself, is basic to what God had in mind
in giving the Torah. (We note, against frequent assumptions,

that these are good Old Testament ideals, not Christian innovations. We also note the difference between the unreserved love of God and the measured love of neighbour – no more, but no less, than one loves one's own sinful self.)

The scribe, musing on this apparently obvious answer, draws the devastating conclusion: this is more than all sacrifices and offerings. Exactly so, replies Jesus; and you are therefore not far from the kingdom of God. Not because you're climbing a ladder of spiritual advancement, but because you've grasped the truth at the heart of Jesus' ministry: Jesus has come to offer, and accomplish, the reality to which the Temple points but which it cannot ultimately deliver. Draw another straight line from here to Hebrews: the blood of bulls and goats can never take away sin. All they can do is to point to that deeper taking away which is accomplished through the death of Jesus.

Why then the Temple? This puzzle, very close to Paul's frequent question as to why God gave the Law, is often answered in terms of religious development: people in earlier days thought they needed animal sacrifices, but we've grown out of such things. That's not the New Testament answer. The Temple was given as a true signpost; there was nothing wrong with it. But the signpost isn't the reality, and if people are mistaking the one for the other the time may come to chop the signpost down.

The question, though, bounces back at today's Church. We don't go in for killing bulls and goats, but do we show evidence of the reality to which their blood was supposed to point? Or have we substituted a new regime of 'dead works' which impede, rather than facilitate, our worship of the living God?

The Third Sunday
Before Advent

—— ∾ ——

Jonah 3.1–5, 10
Hebrews 9.24–28
Mark 1.14–20

'Once, only once, and once for all.' The hymn that starts thus withdraws with the left hand some of what it gives with the right, hinting that Christ's unique sacrifice is still somehow present in the eucharist. This is understandable: every time we stress the uniqueness of Jesus, we risk making him distant, or even irrelevant. All Christian systems of thought have to cope with this question.

But we shouldn't tone down Hebrews' insistence on the one-offness of the sacrifice of Jesus Christ. Hebrews isn't about the eucharist, but about that upon which the eucharist (and everything else) is based. The letter, like the whole New Testament, assumes a Jewish world-view: the story of Israel, in both its sequence and its smaller elements, is the story of how the one true God is dealing with the ruin of humanity, embracing the whole world with forgiveness and hope.

Hebrews 8—10 expounds Jeremiah's prophecy of the new covenant in which sins would be forgiven once for all. That's the point. It draws together earlier themes, focusing on Christ as the high priest who accomplishes, finally, all that the sacrificial system had spoken of. As with birth or marriage,

122

you don't repeat the decisive event; you live by, and within, its consequences. To suggest that Jesus' death needs repeating to be relevant or contemporary is to admit that we haven't understood it.

In the present passage, Christ's death is both like and unlike the Day of Atonement ritual. The high priest disappears into the sanctuary, and reappears to sort out the continuing sin of the people. He'll do it again next year, too. But Christ has gone into the heavenly places, making atonement once for all; his reappearance will not be to deal with sin, but to save those who await his coming. Christian life takes place on the timeline between completed atonement and Jesus' final reappearance.

Theories about atonement are out of fashion at the moment. We prefer straightforward stories like the call of the first disciples: Jesus calls, and Simon, Andrew, James and John obey and follow him. But this isn't as straightforward as it seems. 'The time is fulfilled,' said Jesus, 'and God's kingdom is at hand.' This, too, is a unique moment: history is drawing to its climax. 'Repent, and believe the good news'; the call is not just to work, but to be turned inside out, to reorder priorities, to change direction as well as allegiance. The people of Nineveh repented at Jonah's preaching (perhaps, it is hinted, because they knew of his astonishing rescue from the sea and the fish). Will the people of Israel repent at this seaside prophet, this greater-than-Jonah?

Decisive, one-off challenges are threatening. That's why we turn eschatology into religion, preferring the regular performance of duties to absolute allegiance to the unique Jesus. 'Making the gospel relevant' can sometimes be an excuse for domesticating it, not only in eucharistic theology but in every corner of the Church.

The Second Sunday
Before Advent

——— ∼ ———

Daniel 12.1–3
Hebrews 10.11–14 [15–18] 19–25
Mark 13.1–8

The lady in the icon shop may not have understood my English, let alone my Greek. Did she have an icon of Jesus' resurrection? Yes, she said, pointing at the wall behind her head. There it was, in sequence, preceded by Palm Sunday, the Last Supper, and Calvary, and followed by Ascension and Pentecost.

'But it isn't Jesus' resurrection,' I said; 'that's Jesus raising Adam and Eve at the general resurrection. Haven't you got one of Jesus' *own* resurrection?'

'That is the resurrection,' she said firmly, smiling at my theological incompetence. I smiled back, and bought a smaller one (of Paul).

A typical East/West muddle, and we were of course both right. For the Orthodox, Easter *was* the general resurrection; we may use arm-waving phrases like 'in principle', or 'in a real sense', which mean 'we have to say something like this but we don't quite know how.' We Westerners prefer to separate different historical events, not least (or so we tell ourselves) because the world is still such a sad and wicked place that it doesn't make sense to speak of the resurrection having already happened. (Indeed, 2 Timothy 2.18 warns against such teaching.) But theologically Christ's victory at the first Easter is not different from the victory on the last day. Unless we see Easter like this we diminish it.

The opening verses of Daniel 12, which became the favourite rabbinic text on the resurrection, point in Christian reading *both* to the general resurrection, historically still awaited, *and* to the resurrection of Jesus, following his 'time of anguish' on the cross. New creation began at Easter: Daniel's language about people of dust becoming like the sky and the stars is a way of saying just that. As we move towards the close of the Trinity season (relabelled now as Sundays Before Advent, that is, Sundays Before Sundays Before Christmas), our focus is turned towards the victory of Christ at the cosmic, not only the personal, level.

Within that, of course, the victory is to be seen also as the accomplishment of the new covenant. Hebrews reaches its crowning moment in this passage: Jeremiah's promise is fulfilled (some random electricity seems to have got into the choice of readings, and the selection of verses, at this time of the year). Christian life is designed to take place not in an atmosphere of fear and anxiety about whether God is after all gracious and forgiving, but in the certainty that we have, permanently, that access to God's presence which the Jerusalem Temple both symbolized and restricted.

Jesus and the Temple are thus bound to be set in opposition. If he has spoken and acted truly, there is no room for the signs and symbols which foreshadowed his achievement. But we who still live in a world of wars and rumours of wars may appropriately re-apply his warnings to the time still to come. What are the Temples to be set aside when Easter is finally complete?

Christic the King

—— ∼ ——

Daniel 7.9–10, 13–14
Revelation 1.4b–8
John 18.33b–37

The 'Feast of Christ the King' was invented by Pius XI in 1925. Only in 1970 was it moved from October to the last Sunday before Advent. It slid into Anglicanism very recently, introducing three muddles.

First, the proper feast of Christ the King is Ascension. Any suggestion that Christ only becomes King at the end of a long post-Ascension process is unwarranted.

Second, the idea that 'the kingdom of God' denotes either a purely future reality, or the reality which the saints presently enjoy in heaven (as some liturgies now say), is likewise way off the mark, radically distorting the Bible's kingdom-language.

Third, Advent itself celebrates Christ's second coming and the consummation of all things, not as the end of a process but as a fresh act of grace. Having 'Christ the King' here effects a subtle but radical change in the Church's year, in its implicit story and theology.

Having said all that, one of the great achievements of the current lectionary is its correct reading of Daniel 7 not as the Son of Man 'coming' from heaven to earth, but as his triumphant vindication and exaltation. The direction of travel is up, not down. The Son of Man represents the saints of the Most High, who have suffered at the hands of the beasts and are now rescued and vindicated. This speaks both of the resurrection, ascension and heavenly kingship of Jesus and of the future vindication of the martyrs.

Thus, in Revelation 1 (though a few verses later the Son of Man looks like the Ancient of Days as well), Christ's public vindication is the foundation of the suffering Church's confidence: 'the firstborn of the dead' is in fact 'the ruler of the kings of the earth'. This is the ground both of hope for the future and of political action (including martyrdom) in the present.

We watch the multiple ironies set up by this claim as Jesus stands before Pilate. 'My kingdom is not from this world' doesn't imply that Jesus' sphere of rule is purely heavenly, leaving earth to stew in its own juice. The saying isn't about the kingdom's *location*, but about its *character*: this kingdom isn't the sort that advances by violence. It will come on earth as in heaven, because it is about truth. Pilate, who doesn't know what truth is (do please read half a verse more, and let the famous question hang in the air for a moment), doesn't know that there can be a kingdom without violence.

But we can't really blame him. Even those who name the name of Jesus have taken two millennia to get to the point of imagining that Jesus might really have meant it. As we learn to tell the story right, let's remember that it ends in the embrace of mercy and truth, justice and peace.

The Society for Promoting Christian Knowledge (SPCK) was
founded in 1698. Its mission statement is:

To promote Christian knowledge by

- **Communicating the Christian faith in its
  rich diversity**

- **Helping people to understand the Christian faith
  and to develop their personal faith; and**

- **Equipping Christians for mission and ministry**

SPCK Worldwide serves the Church through Christian
literature and communication projects in 100 countries, and
provides books for those training for ministry in many parts of
the developing world. This worldwide service depends upon the
generosity of others and all gifts are spent wholly on ministry
programmes, without deductions.

SPCK Bookshops support the life of the Christian community
by making available a full range of Christian literature and other
resources, providing support for those training for ministry, and
assisting bookstalls and book agents throughout the UK.

SPCK Publishing produces Christian books and resources,
covering a wide range of inspirational, pastoral, practical and
academic subjects. Authors are drawn from many different
Christian traditions, and publications aim to meet the needs of a
wide variety of readers in the UK and throughout the world.

The Society does not necessarily endorse the individual views
contained in its publications, but hopes they stimulate readers to
think about and further develop their Christian faith.

For information about the Society, visit our website at
www.spck.org.uk, or write to:
SPCK, Holy Trinity Church, Marylebone Road,
London NW1 4DU, United Kingdom.

Breinigsville, PA USA
03 October 2010
246590BV00004B/14/P